D0197826

# A Field Guide to Ticks

## Help Us Keep This Guide Up to Date

Every effort has been made by the author and editors to make this guide as accurate and useful as possible. However, many things can change after a guide is published—science progresses, regulations change, techniques evolve, facilities come under new management, and so on.

We welcome your comments concerning your experiences with this guide and how you feel it could be improved and kept up to date. While we may not be able to respond to all comments and suggestions, we'll take them to heart, and we'll also make certain to share them with the author. Please send your comments and suggestions to the following address:

The Globe Pequot Press
Reader Response/Editorial Department
P.O. Box 480
Guilford, CT 06437

Or you may e-mail us at:
editorial@GlobePequot.com

Thanks for your input, and stay healthy!

# A Field Guide to Ticks

Prevention and Treatment of Lyme Disease and Other
Ailments Caused by Ticks, Scorpions, Spiders, and Mites

Susan Carol Hauser

**FALCON**GUIDES ®

GUILFORD, CONNECTICUT
HELENA, MONTANA

AN IMPRINT OF THE GLOBE PEQUOT PRESS

**FALCON**GUIDES®

Copyright © 2001, 2008 by Susan Carol Hauser
Previously published as *Outwitting Ticks*

Text design by Sheryl P. Kober
Illustrations by Diane Blasius unless otherwise credited

**Library of Congress Cataloging-in-Publication Data**
Hauser, Susan, 1942-
  A field guide to ticks : prevent and treat lyme disease and other ailments caused by ticks, scorpions, spiders, and mites / Susan Carol Hauser. – 2nd ed.
      p. cm.
  Previous ed.: Outwitting ticks, 2001.
  Includes bibliographical references and index.
  ISBN-13: 978-0-7627-4740-5
  1. Tick-borne diseases—United States. 2. Ticks as carriers of disease—United States. 3. Ticks—United States. 4. Lyme disease—United States. I. Title.
  RA641.T5H38 2008
  362.196'968–dc22

                                                2007049924

Printed in the United States of America
10 9 8 7 6 5 4 3 2 1

For Joani Becker, tick wrangler

# Contents

# Preface

My first encounter with ticks—wood ticks, also called dog ticks—was a formative event in my life. I was young, maybe eight years old. I was a city girl, but was visiting my grandparents at their cabin in northern Minnesota. I had my dolls with me, and one day I found the perfect place to play with them: under the high skirt of a massive pine tree. I was happily engrossed in my little-girl-as-mommy fantasy when a neighbor boy, about twelve years old, stopped by. He peered in at me through the branches of my tree. "I wouldn't play under there," he said, in a know-it-all tone.

"Why not?" I countered.

"Wood ticks," was his simple reply.

I didn't know about wood ticks, but he showed them to me. They were crawling all over my arms and legs and clothes, and the arms and legs and clothes of my dolls. I don't remember my exit from the filtered light of my pine-tree world, but I know that nature was not the same for me after that.

In those days, around 1950, nobody liked wood ticks. They were creepy and sneaky and disgusting. But for the most part, our horror was confined to the realm of aesthetics. A tick not immediately discovered on the body glommed onto it and resisted removal. The "bite" itched after the tick was pulled off, sometimes for days. Ticks found on the dog were even worse because they concealed themselves in the dog's fur until they were bloated. Sometimes they remained undetected until they were sated and fell off their host, dropping onto the floor, a large, liver-colored, glistening pearl easily squashed by the bare foot of a child.

In spite of their bad reputation, we considered ticks to be benign. Still, it seemed a bad idea to share blood with one, and in some ways when the saga of the Lyme tick began to unfold in the 1980s, I was not surprised. It was merely confirmation of a niggling fear I'd had since the episode under the pine tree thirty years earlier: Ticks were not just ugly in appearance and behavior; they were dangerous.

Although I was an adult when Lyme disease made headlines, I was not the least bit comforted by the assertion that wood ticks and Lyme ticks were different, and that wood ticks did not carry Lyme disease. After all, they weren't even sure what Lyme disease was; how could they be so confident that wood ticks were not implicated? The news that Lyme ticks, also called deer ticks and blacklegged ticks, were very tiny added to my anxiety, as did the news that deer and mice played some role in the whole Lyme disease pageant.

As an adult I moved to rural northern Minnesota, land of wood ticks and even a Wood Tick Festival, and comforted myself for a long time with the notion that Lyme disease was an East Coast thing. Then we began to hear that you could get Lyme disease in Minnesota. The deer that roamed our yard and the mice in our woodpile were carriers of the Lyme disease germ. I had to come to terms with the vicissitudes of nature. I have been able to do that in large part because I have also come to believe in the old saw that knowledge is power.

A while ago my editor at The Globe Pequot Press called and asked if I would write a book on Lyme disease and related bug-inspired afflictions. *Ewww,* I thought to myself. Ticks. Do I really want to know more? Could I come to love the beauty of a tick kiss, and the elegant survival of a bacterium similar to the one that causes syphilis? Could I muster the courage to look straight on at a detailed drawing of the business end of a tick? Would I forever be glad that I pushed myself down the crooked path of science, or would I forever fear to leave my house?

Did I want the power of knowledge on this subject? My mind said yes; my heart searched for a dolly to cling to. Together, heart and mind, I decided I would sally forth into a microscopic world where there is neither mind nor heart, only survival. Yes, I would write the book. In the end, I find that knowledge is something to cling to, and that it comforts me, as I hope it does you.

# Acknowledgments

My thanks to the following for their contributions to this book:

Steven Clemenson, M.D.

Patrick Guilfoile, Ph.D.

Lori Harms, D.V.M.

# Introduction

In 2001, when this book was first published as *Outwitting Ticks*, the mystery of the origins of Lyme disease and the role of the deer tick, *Ixodes scapularis*, in its transmission were well known. Since then, deer ticks have not changed their habits, nor has the Lyme disease germ, *Borrelia burgdorferi*. Since 1997 Lyme disease cases have been reported in every state with the exception of Montana. In some states it is rare, such as Alaska, Hawaii, Mississippi, North Dakota, South Dakota, and Colorado. In some states, particularly in the Northeast and the Midwest, reported cases generally continue to increase in number (Centers for Disease Control; www.cdc.gov).

The standard and effective treatment for Lyme disease also has not changed much. Antibiotics administered early in the infection usually result in a total cure. Complications are rare. However, the understanding and treatment of what has been called chronic or persistent Lyme disease, or post–Lyme disease syndrome, has changed significantly. When this book first went to press, studies were underway to determine the best treatment for cases that appeared to not be cured by initial antibiotic treatment. These were usually cases not diagnosed until the second or third stage of the disease. Scientists hoped to determine whether or not extended antibiotic treatment provided cure or relief for those with persistent symptoms.

The studies, as reported by the National Institute of Allergy and Infectious Diseases (NIAID, a division of the National Institutes of Health; www.nih.niaid.gov), determined that long-term antibiotic treatment does not necessarily improve the health or well-being of persons with what is now called post-treatment chronic Lyme disease (PTCLD). NIAID notes at www3.niaid.nih.gov that "it is unclear whether such symptoms are due to a long-term persistent infection or other causes." On a more hopeful note, the Web site reports on successful treatment of PTCLD pain using a neuropathic drug. It also notes that the complete genome for *Borrelia burgdorferi* has been sequenced by scientists at the Institute for Genomic Research (J. Craig Venter Institute) and that "the application of this information will play a significant role in increasing our understanding of the pathogenesis of Lyme disease at the molecular and cellular levels. . . ." This knowledge should also contribute to the development of improved diagnostic tests. Currently, the observation of clinical symptoms remains the primary diagnostic tool for Lyme disease.

Now, as before, the best defense against Lyme disease is prevention and, failing that, early diagnosis and treatment. The habits and habitats of ticks explained in this book will help you to prevent infection. Symptoms of Lyme disease and its progress are also described. If you think you have the symptoms and have been in deer tick country, seek medical attention, and let the practitioner know that you might have been exposed to Lyme disease.

*Chapter 1*
# The Lyme Disease Saga

Lyme disease is a multisystem infection that has claimed the attention of outdoor lovers and rural and suburban dwellers in the United States and Europe. It is caused by a bacterium, *Borrelia burgdorferi*, and is transmitted to humans by blacklegged ticks. Its incidence is primarily restricted to the Northeast, Midwest, and Pacific Northwest of the United States, and to Europe. Those bare facts belie the complexity of the disease and the intricacies of its diagnosis and treatment. The story of Lyme disease is a long one and, though our efforts are great, its end is not yet written.

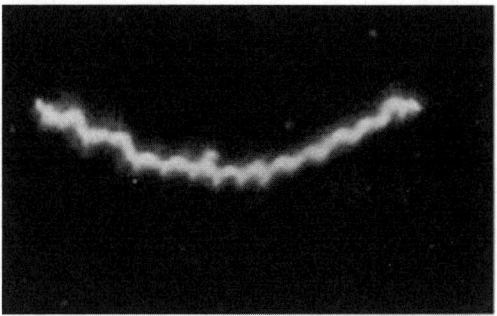

*Borrelia burgdorferi* as seen through a darkfield microscope.
National Institutes of Health; used with permission.

## Players in the Lyme Disease Saga
### The Germ

*Borrelia burgdorferi* is a spirochete, an infectious bacterium that causes Lyme disease in humans and other animals.

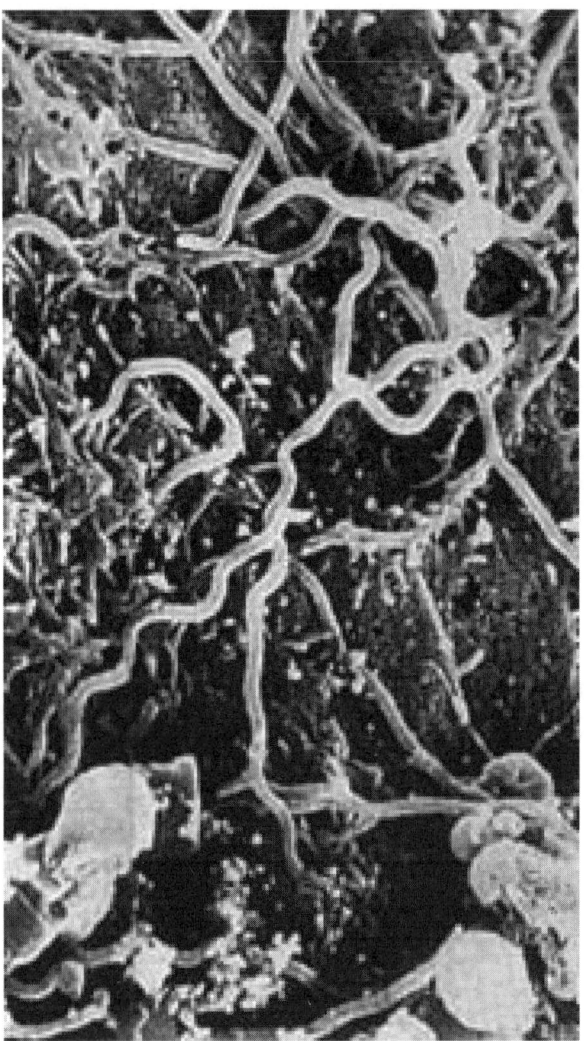

The spaghetti-like forms shown are *Borrelia burgdorferi* isolated from the midgut of a deer tick. This magnified image of the spirochetes was taken with an electron microscope. National Institutes of Health; used with permission.

Spirochetes, including the one that causes syphilis, are known for their ability to migrate deep into the body, where the body's immune response and antibiotics do not easily reach. Unlike Lyme disease, the syphilis spirochete does not have a nonhuman vector, but is transferred directly from human to human.

Survival is not easy for a bacterium like *Borrelia burgdorferi*. First, it needs someplace to live—a host reservoir with an immune system that does not kill it. Second, in return, it must not kill the host, else its life will end too. Third, since the host is bound to die someday, *B. burgdorferi* needs another host, a vector, to be a Good Samaritan and carry it to another host reservoir so it does not die off with the first one.

Today, after centuries and probably millennia of trial-and-error living, *B. burgdorferi* has a well established life cycle, complete with compatible host reservoirs, including mice, and Good Samaritans, commonly known as deer or Lyme ticks, but properly called blacklegged ticks.

## Vectors

A vector is an organism that carries disease-causing microorganisms from one host to another. For example, blacklegged ticks are vectors for Lyme disease because they carry *B. burgdorferi* from mice to humans. They are described in detail in Chapter 2.

## Hosts

A host in nature is an animal or plant on which, or in which, another organism lives, either permanently or temporarily. For example, ticks host *B. burgdorferi*. Mice, deer, and sometimes humans host ticks. Ticks have the dubious distinction of both being hosts (to *B. burgdorferi*) and utilizing hosts (including mice and humans).

### Host Reservoirs: Competent and Incompetent

A host reservoir is a host in which a parasite, such as *B. burgdorferi,* thrives, and from which it is transmitted to other host reservoirs. For example, the white-footed mouse *Peromyscus leucopus* is a host reservoir for *B. burgdorferi,* as are other mice, rats, and similar woodland creatures, including chipmunks and birds. Some hosts of the ticks, however, are not considered to be host reservoirs for the *B. burgdorferi* because they do not contribute to its replication or distribution in nature.

The white-tailed deer, *Odocoileus virginianus,* and humans, for example, may be hosts to *B. burgdorferi* (as well as to ticks), but are not host reservoirs. Although *B. burgdorferi* can live in them, they are not considered host reservoirs because they are incompetent hosts. The germ does not flourish in them, and vectors do not transfer the germ from them to another host. For example, an adult tick may get *B. burgdorferi* from a deer, but as the adult meal is the tick's last one, it will not be passing the germ on to a subsequent host. The failure of a germ to flourish in a given creature may be due to natural immunity, or to an environment in the creature that is not successful for the germ.

Although white-tailed deer are not good host reservoirs for *B. burgdorferi,* they are the preferred mating site for blacklegged ticks. They are, therefore, important for—perhaps critical to—creation of the ticks and thus are indirectly important to the survival of *B. burgdorferi* and to the transmission of Lyme disease.

## Outer Surface Proteins (Osp) and the Lyme Disease Vaccine

Outer surface proteins are expressed on the outside of microorganisms, including *B. burgdorferi*. They are important to understanding Lyme disease because while *B. burgdorferi* is in the gut of a tick it expresses Osp A, but by the time it has migrated to the tick's salivary glands, it has suppressed Osp A and is secreting mostly Osp C. Outer surface proteins are one of the targets of naturally occurring antibodies in humans.

### Antibiotics

Antibiotics are usually a successful defense against *B. burgdorferi*. Early in the disease, when the germ is primarily in the skin and blood, antibiotics are a highly successful treatment. When Lyme disease has disseminated in the body, reaching well-protected organs such as the brain, cure is more difficult, because antibiotics do not have *B. burgdorferi*'s skill for penetrating organs. However, new research indicates that long-term treatment with antibiotics is no more effective than treatment with placebos.[1]

## The Story: Identification of the Cause of Lyme Disease

*Ixodes* ticks have been biting people for a long time, and there is evidence that they have been giving people Lyme disease for more than a century, and maybe for millennia, not only in North America but in Europe and Asia. Recent reports also indicate the presence of Lyme disease in South America,[2] and of *Ixodes scapularis* ticks in Mexico.[3]

Although Lyme disease would be named in 1981 in the United States, scientists and physicians in Europe were on its trail long before that. Descriptions of Lyme disease symptoms occur in European medical literature as early as 1883, with numerous later mentions. In fact, prior to the identification of *Borrelia burgdorferi* as the causative agent for Lyme disease, European patients with Lyme symptoms, including the classic bull's-eye rash and flu-like symptoms, were diagnosed with erythema migrans, sometimes called erythema chronicum migrans and commonly referred to as EM. In the 1970s the diagnosis of erythema migrans was made for a number of cases in the United States.[4] Erythema migrans is a descriptive term for the bull's-eye rash that develops in about 80 percent of people who come down with Lyme disease. "Erythema" comes from the Greek word for "red"; "migrans" from the Latin word for "migratory."

By mid-twentieth century scientists and physicians in Europe were not only diagnosing erythema migrans, but were moving in on the cause of the disease. They had associated erythema migrans with the bite of *Ixodes* ticks, and believed erythema migrans was caused by a bacteria because it responded to treatment with penicillin. They were also on the track of *Borrelia burgdorferi* itself. *B. burgdorferi* is a spirochete, a corkscrew-shaped bacterium. It was already known that ticks carried spirochete bacteria, in addition to the bacteria rickettsiae and viruses. The tick-borne spirochete that causes relapsing fever was identified in 1868.[5] Tests, however, failed to reveal the presence of a rickettsial agent or a virus in erythema migrans patients, and in general, patients with rickettsiae did not respond to treatment with penicillin, as did patients with erythema migrans symptoms.

While the erythema migrans story unfolded in Europe, a similar story began to take shape in the United States. In 1975, a group of concerned parents in and around Lyme, Connecticut, contacted the Connecticut State Health Department. They felt that an unusually large number of children had been diagnosed with inflammatory arthritis, and some with the rare and noncontagious juvenile rheumatoid arthritis. Research on the phenomenon was conducted at Yale University in 1975 and 1976. "What emerged was a picture of a multisystem disease that evolved over weeks to months, probably associated with an infectious agent transmitted through a tick bite and associated with prominent immunilogical [sic] phenomenon," according to Daniel Rahn and Janine Evans, authors of *Lyme Disease*.[6]

The relationship of the disease to erythema migrans in Europe and the United States was evident, but by the end of the Yale study it was clear that the bull's-eye rash was only one feature of a complicated disease, and the name was changed to Lyme disease. In 1992 the international medical community, in response to a survey conducted by Dr. Willy Burgdorfer, medical entomologist, agreed to call infection with *B. burgdorferi* "Lyme disease." It is still occasionally referred to as Lyme Borreliosis, after *burgdorferi*'s genus *Borrelia*.

As scientists homed in on the Lyme disease diagnosis, they struggled to identify the specific tick that carried the bacterium, and to isolate the bacterium itself. Both goals were accomplished in the early 1980s. *Ixodes scapularis* were first identified in the Lyme, Connecticut, region. The bacterium *Borrelia burgdorferi* was isolated by Dr. Burgdorfer at the National Institutes of Health, Rocky Mountain Laboratories in Hamilton, Montana. He found them in the guts of *Ixodes scapularis* on Long Island, New York. At the same time in 1981, scientists in Germany were connecting the Lyme disease agent to other *Borrelia* species. In Europe, Burgdorfer's discovery was acted upon quickly and strains of *B. burgdorferi* were isolated from patients with erythema migrans. In 1984 the spirochete was officially named after Burgdorfer.

Following identification of the germ that causes Lyme disease, scientists continued to move forward, searching for a preventative vaccine. Other scientists started looking back: Paleoanthropologists and paleopathologists are now considering the possibility that prehistoric cultures might also have suffered from Lyme disease. Bones from individuals who lived 2,000 years ago that had been diagnosed, in the early 1990s, with rheumatoid arthritis are being reviewed, and evidence indicates the likelihood of *B. burgdorferi* infection.[7]

## Lyme Disease Statistics*

- Lyme disease now accounts for more than 95 percent of all reported vector-borne illness in the United States.

- The number of reported cases has increased twenty-five-fold since national surveillance began in 1982. Approximately 12,500 cases were reported annually by states to the CDC from 1993 to 1997. The CDC reports current annual cases averaging about 15,000 per year.

- Overall incident rate is 5 per 100,000 people, reaching 1 to 3 percent in some highly endemic communities.

- Significant risk of infection in the United States is found in only about one hundred counties in ten states (see Lyme-Endemic States chart, page 9) located along the northeastern and mid-Atlantic seaboard, in the upper north-central region, and in a few counties in northern California.

- Based on CDC criteria, including the description of the erythema migrans rash, musculoskeletal, nervous system, and cardiovascular symptoms, and other criteria such as exposure to tick habitat, cases have been reported to the CDC in all states and the District of Columbia.

- Lyme disease is rarely, if ever, fatal.

- The highest reported rates of Lyme disease are in children two to fifteen years old, and in adults aged thirty to thirty-five.

*Centers for Disease Control and Prevention; Food and Drug Administration*

## Lyme-Endemic States*

| State (For a list of distribution by county, contact a state's health department, or visit their Web site) | Total Number of Cases Reported 1989–1998 | Annual Incidence per 100,000 Persons |
|---|---|---|
| New York | 39,370 | 21.6 |
| Connecticut | 17,728 | 54.2 |
| Pennsylvania | 14,870 | 12.3 |
| New Jersey | 13,428 | 16.9 |
| Wisconsin | 4,760 | 9.3 |
| Rhode Island | 3,717 | 37.5 |
| Maryland | 3,410 | 6.8 |
| Massachusetts | 2,712 | 4.5 |
| Minnesota | 1,745 | 3.8 |
| Delaware | 1,003 | 14.0 |

*Lyme disease is the leading cause of vector-borne infectious illness in the U.S. with about 15,000 cases reported annually, though the disease is greatly under-reported. Based on reported cases, during the past ten years 90 percent of cases of Lyme disease occurred in ten states. Centers for Disease Control and Prevention, "Lyme Disease: Epidemiology."

## Comforting Information

- Even in endemic areas, tick season is short—about three to four months out of each year.

- Only 1.2 percent of persons with recognized [Lyme] tick bites develop Lyme disease, probably because they removed the tick before it had time to transmit the disease (usually within 24 hours of attachment).[8]

- Most people who get Lyme disease and receive appropriate antibiotic treatment recover completely, though symptoms may linger for some months.

- Allen Steere, author of *Lyme Disease,* notes that ". . . even patients with chronic arthritis rarely have continual joint inflammation for longer than several years."[9]

# Chapter 2

# Blacklegged Ticks

Although *Borrelia burgdorferi* is ultimately responsible for Lyme disease in humans, it is not the microbe itself that captures our attention. That honor falls to blacklegged ticks. As the only certain known vector for—transmitter of—*B. burgdorferi* to hosts, such as humans, the ticks are our point of contact with the disease. Understanding them is more important to most of us than understanding the lifestyle of the germ itself.

## Identification of Blacklegged Ticks

In general, blacklegged ticks look like other ticks: They are teardrop-shaped and have eight legs, although the larvae have six legs. Their nubbin heads are not really heads; they have rudimentary eyes and sophisticated mouthparts. They are, however, sensitive to warmth and have a keen sense of chemicals: They are attracted to carbon dioxide, which is how they detect humans and other mammals coming along a path.

Blacklegged ticks differ from dog ticks (*Dermacentor variabilis*), also called wood ticks, in several ways. Most evident is size: Dog ticks are respectably measurable, about 3 to 4 millimeters wide and a bit longer. An adult blacklegged tick is half that size, the size of a sesame seed, or about 2 millimeters. A blacklegged nymph is the size of a poppy seed, about 1 millimeter, and less than half the size of an adult. However, an engorged adult blacklegged tick can be as large as an unengorged dog tick, about the size of two sesame seeds.

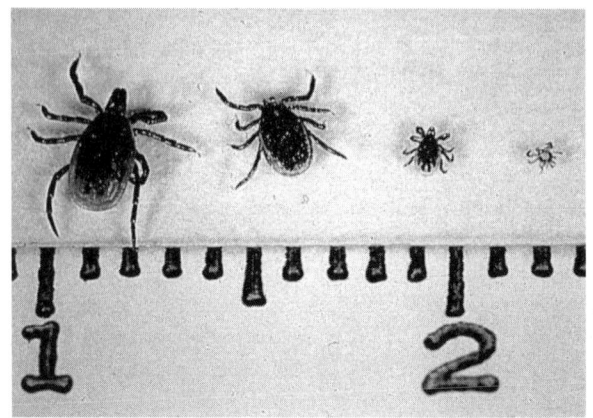

From left to right: The deer tick or blacklegged tick *(Ixodes scapularis),* adult female, adult male, nymph, and larva on a centimeter scale. Centers for Disease Control and Prevention; used with permission.

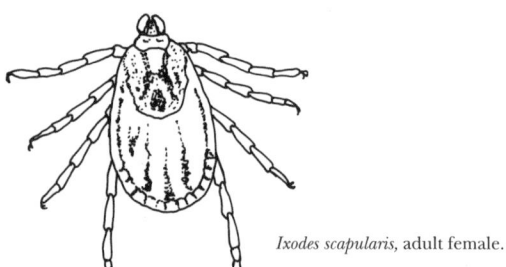

*Ixodes scapularis,* adult female.

Blacklegged ticks and dog ticks also have different color markings, which can best be detected with a magnifying glass. The blacklegged tick is brown or black with eight black legs, and has an orange-red crescent on its back (dorsal shield). An adult dog tick is brown with white markings on its back, and its underside is tan or has brown spots. Differences in anal grooves, posterior festoons, and other features can be detected with a microscope. The pre-anal groove is the main distinguishing feature of genus *Ixodes* ticks.

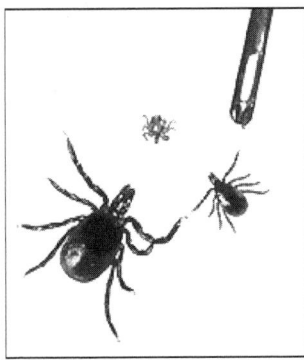

*Ixodes* ticks are much smaller than the common dog and cattle ticks. In their larval and nymphal stages, they are no bigger than the eye of a common sewing needle. Adult ticks are larger, about the size of a small apple seed. Photo by R. Johnson. Centers for Disease Control and Prevention; used with permission.

There are two recognized species of blacklegged ticks in North America: *Ixodes scapularis,* the blacklegged tick, and *Ixodes pacificus,* the western blacklegged tick. Some scientists recognize a third species, *Ixodes dammini,* sometimes called the eastern deer tick, but most agree that the differences between *I. dammini* and *I. scapularis* do not warrant species distinction, and ticks formerly labeled as *dammini* are now called *scapularis.* Even *I. scapularis* and *I. pacificus* are distinct from each other in features only scientists can really care about, including differences in scutum body parts. To the human eye the ticks look the same. What is important is that both species are carriers of Lyme disease, and both bite humans.

### Tick Vectors of *B. burgdorferi**

| Tick Species | Location | Percentage Infected with *B. burgdorferi* |
|---|---|---|
| *Ixodes scapularis* | Eastern and upper midwestern United States | 0–75 percent |
| *Ixodes pacificus* | West Coast United States | 2–5 percent |
| *Ixodes ricinus* | Europe | 0–75 percent |
| *Ixodes persulcatus* | Asia | Unknown |
| *Amblyomma americanum* | Southern and eastern United States (The association of *A. americanum* and Lyme disease has not been fully determined.) | 0–5 percent |

*\*B. burgdorferi* is not transmitted from person to person (April 30, 2000; www.cdc. gov), nor is it transmitted by flies, fleas, or lice, although there is some indication that it might, though extremely rarely, be transmitted by the bite of some flies (Anderson, p. 226).

*Atlas of Infections of the Skin* (Aly, p. 164); used with permission.

### Classification of the Blacklegged Ticks That Carry Lyme Disease

    **Kingdom:** Animal (others include plant and fungi)
    **Phylum:** Arthropoda (others include Chordata)
    **Class:** Arachnida (others include Insecta)
    **Subclass:** Acarina (others include Scorpionomorphae)
    **Order:** Parasitiformes (others include Arachnida)
    **Suborder:** Ixodida (sometimes Metastigmata)
        (others include Astigmata)
    **Family:** *Ixodidae* (others include Argasidae)

**Genus:** *Ixodes* (others include Dermacentor)
**Species:** *Scapularis* (eastern North America) and
      *pacificus* (western North America) (others
      include *ricinus* in Europe and *persulcatus* in Asia)

## Comments on the Classification

Creatures in the phylum Arthropoda have exoskeletons (external) and other common features. That's clear enough, but there are several opportunities for confusion in understanding the taxonomic classification of black-legged ticks:

- The class Arachnida is divided into orders that include Arachnida (including spiders); Parasitiformes (including ticks); and Acarina (including some mites). The use of the name Arachnida for both the class and one order in the class makes it easy to think that ticks are spiders; in fact, they split off from each other at the class designation and are only second cousins.

- The order Parasitiformes has a suborder Ixodida Metastigmata (whose families include Ixodidae, hard ticks, and Argasidae, soft ticks. Blacklegged ticks are hard ticks.

- The genus Ixodes shares its name with its family, Ixodidae. The genus Ixodes includes the two black-legged tick species, *I. scapularis* and *I. pacificus,* that carry Lyme disease in North America. It also includes *Ixodes ricinus,* the carrier of Lyme disease in Europe, and *Ixodes persulcatus,* an Asian tick known to carry *B. burgdorferi,* although it is not known if the tick transmits Lyme disease to people. A tick of another family, the Lone Star tick, *Amblyomma americanum,* is known to carry *B. burgdorferi,* but it has not yet been proven to transmit Lyme disease (Aly, p. 164).

## Life Stages and Life Cycle of Blacklegged Ticks

The tick life pageant takes two years to complete, although it can take as long as five years; if a host is not found, nymphal and adult ticks are able to overwinter an extra year and maybe more. In the usual cycle, eggs hatch in the spring as larvae. In the summer, the larvae take blood meals and molt into nymphs, then overwinter. In the next spring or early summer, the nymphs take a blood meal and molt into male and female adults. The female adults mate in the fall on a host, take a blood meal that usually lasts from nine to eleven days, fall off, and lie dormant in leaf litters through the winter. In the next spring (year one of a new cycle) they lay their eggs and then die. After mating in the fall, the male ticks tend to stay on the host.

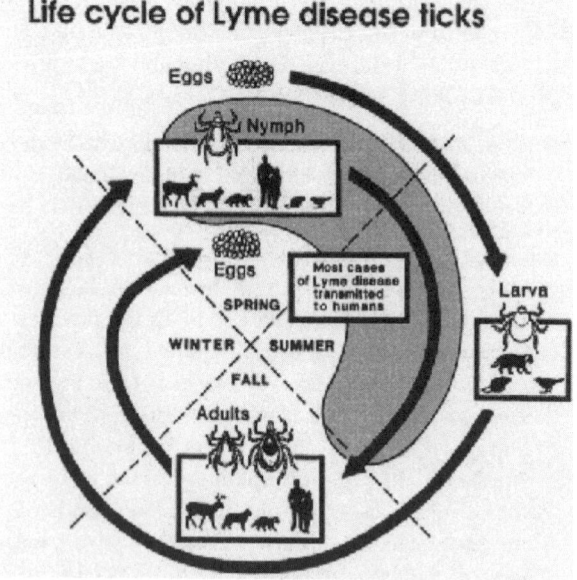

Centers for Disease Control and Prevention; used with permission.

They may mate with other females, and may take sporadic blood meals. Male adult ticks do not feed long enough to transfer *B. burgdorferi* to the host and are not considered vectors for Lyme disease.

## Behavior of Blacklegged Ticks

While blacklegged ticks can and do crawl, they do not jump onto potential hosts, nor do they free-fall onto them. They contact their hosts by "questing" for them, a scientific term for lying-in-wait. At all three stages, larva, nymph, and adult, blacklegged ticks set themselves up on a blade of grass or other prop, hang on with their back legs, and hold out their front legs. When an appropriate host brushes by, one that exudes warmth and carbon dioxide, which the tick senses with an organ in its front legs (Hallers organ), the tick lets go of its perch and latches onto its new host.

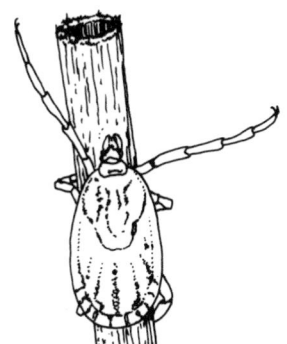

A tick "questing" for a host. Ticks do not jump or fall from trees. They rarely climb more than 3 feet from the ground on vegetation. We find them in the hair on our heads because they have climbed us looking for a suitable location to settle in.

A tick tends to climb against gravity. It might attach at the site of contact, or move about until it meets an obstacle. It usually seeks a spot on its host where it is less likely

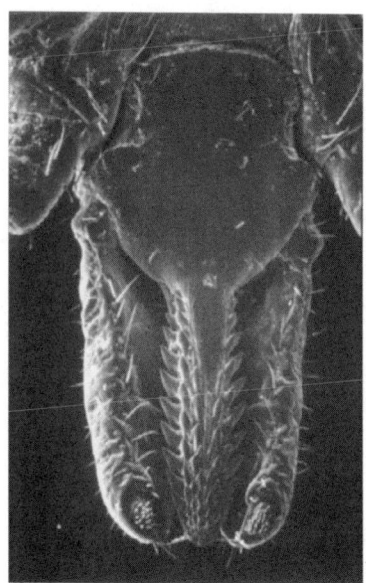

Mouthparts of a tick. The palps spread out to the sides when the tick inserts the hypostome into the skin of the host. The backward-pointing barbs on the hypostome help keep the tick attached while it feeds. Centers for Disease Control and Prevention; used with permission.

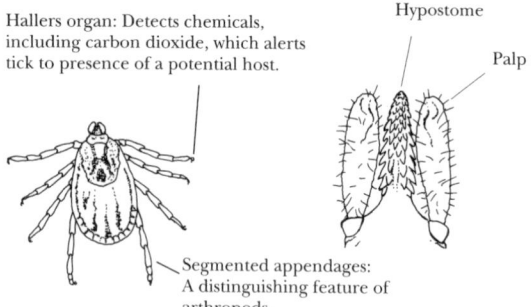

Hallers organ: Detects chemicals, including carbon dioxide, which alerts tick to presence of a potential host.

Hypostome

Palp

Segmented appendages: A distinguishing feature of arthropods.

to be detected, for instance in hair or folds of skin. Once it has found a suitable location, it sets about obtaining its meal. First it secretes a sort of cement that adheres it to the host—that is why an attached tick is difficult to remove. It then uses its mouthparts to create a little well in the skin of the host. Blood collects there, and the tick drinks it. As part of the process, according to "Tick-Transmitted Diseases in Humans," "Excess water extracted from the ingested blood is voided back into the host through the salivary glands. Hence ticks, especially the nymph and adult stages, are efficient transmitters of pathogens."[1] When the tick is sated and engorged, it falls off.

Mice and deer hosts are useful to blacklegged ticks at different stages of tick development. The larvae and nymphs are very small and do not get about easily. Therefore they are more likely to attach themselves to small mammals, such as mice, which frequent the leaf litter where the tick eggs hatch. Adult ticks prefer deer as hosts. Deer offer a more suitable blood meal in terms of quantity, and the adult tick, which is larger than the larva and the nymph, climbs higher on vegetation than larvae and nymphs, where it is able to catch onto and climb the limbs of deer. Once on board, the adults mate and take their final blood meals.

## Transmission of Lyme Disease by Blacklegged Ticks

Blacklegged ticks take three blood meals in their life cycle, one for each stage of development: larva, nymph, and adult. If, during a larval or nymphal meal, which typically lasts three to five days each, the tick acquires *B. burgdorferi*, it can pass the germ on to the host of its next meal. For instance, if a larva, which looks just like an adult except it is very, very small, feasts on a mouse that has *B. burgdorferi*, when the larva takes its next meal, as a nymph, it can pass the germ on to the host of the nymphal meal. Larvae and nymphs both feed on mice and other small creatures (some 119 hosts have been identified),[2] and these unwitting hosts can be host for many larvae and nymphs, so the germ is easily passed around.

If a tick does not acquire *B. burgdorferi* until its second meal, during the nymphal stage, it is less likely to pass the germ on to a human during its third meal as an adult. Adult ticks usually take their meals in the late fall when humans do not frequent the woods, and do not sport much exposed skin. The ticks also seem to prefer the larger blood supply of the deer for their final repast, and for their mating site. An adult tick that acquires *B. burgdorferi* from a deer poses no threat to humans as the adult meal is the last one, and it appears that transmission of *B. burgdorferi* to the tick eggs is extremely rare if not impossible.

It is the bite of a nymph that offers humans the most risk of infection with *B. burgdorferi*. A larva supping on a human could not pass on Lyme disease because the larval meal is the tick's first one, and it could not yet have acquired the disease. The tick that acquires the disease during that first blood meal is most likely to pass the germ on to a human who serves as host for the second-stage (nymphal) blood meal. A nymph that takes its second meal from an infected host could acquire the germ and potentially pass it on to the human who serves as the blood source for the third meal. However, adult black-legged ticks do not commonly bite humans because the third meal takes place in late fall when humans are less likely to be out and about in tick habitat. Further, adult ticks are less plentiful than nymphs.

## Habitat, Distribution, and Emergence of Blacklegged Ticks

Blacklegged ticks might appear to be everywhere these days, but they are actually quite fussy about where they live.

### Prime Habitat for Lyme Disease Vectors

- High-humidity environs (e.g., riverine, estuarial, and coastal habitat).

- Shaded, damp, forested, and brushy areas covered with leaf litter.

- Areas frequented by deer: woodlots, wooded areas between yards, edges between yards, and wooded or unmaintained brushy areas.

- Areas frequented by mice and chipmunks (e.g., around woodpiles, stone walls, unkempt brushy areas, and tall grass at edges of residential properties).

- Brushy and grassy areas along hiking trails in areas frequented by deer.

- Bayberry, scrub oak, and other scrub habitat in northeastern coastal fringe areas.

- Oak-woodland chaparral ground cover habitats of coastal northern California.

These considerations explain why Lyme disease is prevalent in the northeastern United States and in Minnesota and Wisconsin, but they do not explain the low incidence of Lyme disease in southern and western regions that lay claim to many of these conditions. However, the transmission of the infectious agent to humans is dependent on several factors. Not only must there be blacklegged ticks, but the ticks must carry *B. burgdorferi*.

The larval stage of western blacklegged ticks, *Ixodes pacificus,* and blacklegged ticks, *Ixodes scapularis,* that live in the southern and southeastern United States tend to feed on lizards and other vertebrates that are not susceptible to infection with *B. burgdorferi. B. burgdorferi* does exist in nature in these areas, but it tends to survive in vectors that do not bite humans.[3]

Although there is evidence that Lyme disease has been around for a long time, it is only in the last several decades that it has emerged as a major health threat.

According to the Centers for Disease Control, reported cases of Lyme disease in the U.S. have increased "about [twenty-five-fold] since national surveillance began in 1982," with a mean of about 12,500 cases reported annually from 1993 to 1997. More recently the CDC indicated an average of 15,000 cases are reported annually.[4]

Current popular and scientific literature on Lyme disease generally agrees on the cause of the emergence of this disease both in North America and in Europe: It is the result of increased populations of deer, which has resulted in increased populations of blacklegged ticks, the only known vector that successfully transmits Lyme disease to humans.

The increase in deer populations has been attributed to a sequence of events profitable to deer. Allen C. Steere, a Lyme disease expert, explains the process in a chapter in *Emerging Infections.* He reports that the sequence began about 15,000 years ago with the withdrawal of glaciers from what is now the northeast and midwestern United States. The retreating glaciers left terminal moraine tundra in their wake, which eventually developed into forests that were heavily populated with deer. He cites descriptions of colonial New England that "include comments about the abundance of deer and annoying ticks."[5]

## Active Seasons for Blacklegged Ticks in Endemic Lyme Areas (Northeastern, Midwestern, and West Coast United States)

| Stage of Tick Development | Season Active | Potential Hosts for *B. burgdorferi* | Feeding Period | Importance for Humans | Recommended Action to Avoid Infection |
|---|---|---|---|---|---|
| Larva | *I. scapularis:* late May, June, early July; *I. pacificus:* March–June | Mice; other small mammals and vertebrates; humans | 3–5 days | Not important: do not carry *B. burgdorferi* until acquired with nymphal blood meal | None |
| Nymph | *I. scapularis:* late July, August, early September; *I. pacificus:* March–June | Mice; other small mammals and vertebrates; humans | 3–5 days | Extremely important: Nymphs carry *B. burgdorferi* if it was acquired during larval blood meal; a nymph can pass it on to the host of nymphal blood meal, including humans who frequent tick territory during this time period, and are dressed for warm weather (i.e., skin exposed) | • Avoid tick habitat<br>• Wear protective clothing<br>• Use tick repellent<br>• Check for ticks<br>• Remove attached ticks with care<br>• Be alert for Lyme disease symptoms<br>• Consider vaccination |
| Adult | *I. scapularis:* October–December, sometimes March into May; *I. pacificus:* November–May | Deer; humans | 9–11 days | Somewhat important: Adults carry *B. burgdorferi* if acquired during larval or nymphal blood meal but are unlikely to bite humans, in part because humans tend not to be in tick territory, and are well clothed when out; some evidence indicates that most tick bites in the South might be from adult ticks | • Wear protective clothing<br>• Use tick repellent<br>• Check for ticks<br>• Remove attached ticks with care<br>• Be alert for Lyme disease symptoms |

Centers for Disease Control and Prevention

According to Steere, the population of deer in these northeast regions was reduced dramatically during the eighteenth and nineteenth centuries when the woods were converted to farmlands and "deer were hunted practically to extinction." In the early twentieth century, as farmland opened in the West, forests reestablished themselves in the Northeast, as did deer populations. Deer also thrived because their natural predators, such as wolves, had been hunted to near extinction, and because of environmental efforts that protected deer habitat. The same habitat considerations likely contributed to the increase of deer in Minnesota and Wisconsin.[6]

Steere notes that deer are not the only requirement for the sustenance of Lyme disease in an area. "Other factors, such as rodent populations, vegetation, temperature, and humidity, must also play an important role in the ecology of the disease."[7] These requirements include competent reservoir hosts and, for the transmission of Lyme disease to humans, vectors that bite humans.

*Chapter 3*
# Lyme Disease

Sorting out the details of the transmission of Lyme disease can be challenging, but no less so than sorting out the details of the disease itself. The knowledge we have gained to date has brought relief to many; the knowledge we are sure to gain in the future will bring relief to many more.

## Infection

Although mice, deer, and blacklegged ticks get most of the attention for Lyme disease, the real culprit is the microscopic germ, *Borrelia burgdorferi,* a bacterium species of the family Spirochaetaceae. Three species of *B. burgdorferi* have been recognized to date: *Borrelia burgdorferi* (species), in North America and Europe, and *Borrelia garinii* and *Borrelia afzelii,* to date found only in Europe. Because each of these species exists in multiple strains, having

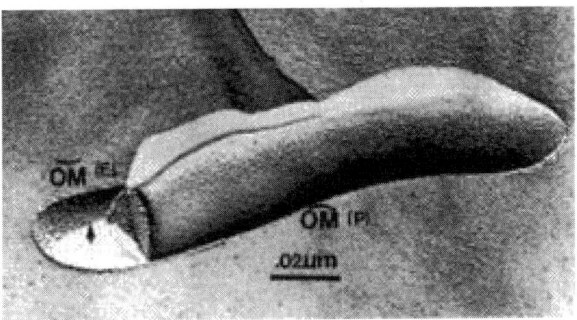

Close-up picture of the Lyme bacterium produced by freeze fracture electron microscopy. This process allows researchers to split apart two membranes that make up the microbe's coat. They can then study the proteins (see arrow) that make up the coat to understand the organism and improve vaccine design, diagnostic testing, and treatment for Lyme disease. National Institutes of Health; used with permission.

Lyme disease once does not necessarily protect one from infection with a different strain.

---

**Taxonomic Classification**

Order: Spirochaetales
Family: Spirochaetaceae

| | |
|---|---|
| Genus: *Treponoma* | Genus: *Borrelia* |
| Species: *T. pallidum* | Species: *B. burgdorferi sensu lato*† |
| (causes syphilis) | (causes Lyme disease) |
| | Strains: |
| | *B. burgdorferi sensu stricto*\* |
| | *B. afzelii* |
| | *B. garinii* |

\* *Sensu lato* refers to the broader category, *sensu stricto* to a category within the broader one (Aly, p. 163).

---

Spirochetes (also spelled spirochaetes) get their name from their corkscrew shape. They move with an undulating and propeller-like motion that allows them to wiggle around in the small spaces between the cells of their hosts. Spirochetes cannot be seen with the naked eye. According to Alan G. Barbour, M.D., "A microscope that magnifies at least a hundred times is needed. . . . Even then, the spirochete's extremely narrow width requires special optics or stains to make it visible."[1]

*B. burgdorferi* is passed from a blacklegged tick to a human when a nymph-stage (or sometimes adult) tick "bites" a human in order to take a blood meal. *B. burgdorferi* bacteria in the gut of a tick undergo a change in gene expression that allows them to journey to the tick's salivary glands. During that process, *B. burgdorferi* suppresses production of the outer surface protein A (Osp A) and increases production of Osp C. This process and the journey to the salivary glands usually takes at least twenty-four hours, and during that time the tick does not usually infect its host with *B. burgdorferi.*

Not long ago it was thought that *B. burgdorferi,* in addition to entering the host through tick saliva, might also enter through regurgitation of the tick's gut content into the host. However, that theory is now questioned, as recent knowledge indicates that mostly Osp A is expressed in the gut, while Osp C is expressed in the salivary glands. It is believed that ". . . Osp C is critical for dissemination and transmission of the Lyme spirochete during tick feeding."[2]

While the tick feeds, it inoculates the tissue of the host with saliva and, if infected itself, with *B. burgdorferi.* Once in the host's body, the infection spreads through the skin, the lymph, and the blood. In 80 percent or more of cases, the infection causes a red skin rash. The round "target" rash moves out from the bite in rings, which reflect the action of the bacteria and the body's immune response: As the bacteria feed on sugars, fats, and other substances in the host, they multiply and then compete for food. As their numbers increase, they search for food by moving away from the original bite site. Their motion is visible in the concentric circles of the rash, marked by red and whitish rings. The red areas indicate inflammation caused by the body's immune response to the germ. The whitish areas are those where few of the microbes remain.

Eventually, if they are not eliminated by the body's immune response or by antibiotic medications, *B. burgdorferi* can enter the bloodstream and travel to other organs of the body. Once out of the bloodstream, *B. burgdorferi* is harder to treat because it is more out of reach of the body's immune response and of administered antibiotics.

For a time after the identification of *B. burgdorferi* as the cause of Lyme disease, the effect of Lyme disease on human fetuses was unknown. Because syphilis, also caused by a spirochete, is "associated with stillbirth and with congenital malformations in live-born infants,"[3] there was concern that similar effects might result in infants born to mothers with Lyme disease. Although there is evidence that Lyme disease may pass to a fetus from a mother during pregnancy, two recent studies indicate that fetuses appear not to be at risk for congenital defects caused by Lyme disease.[4] However, according to Helayne M. Silver, M.D., "as the disease is uncommon, and anomalies less common, larger epidemiological studies are required for a definitive resolution to the question of fetal risks with perinatal infection."[5] Furthermore, a pregnant woman with Lyme disease must be "treated with an antibiotic that will not affect the pregnancy."[6]

Lyme disease is described as having three stages:

*Early infection*
- Stage one: localized infection

- Stage two: disseminated infection

*Late infection*
- Stage three: persistent infection

Although the labels occasionally may vary (for example, stage one might be called "early infection" rather than "localized infection"), the distinctions are clear: Stage one refers to symptoms that occur within a few weeks of a bite and are limited to the characteristic rash and flu-like symptoms; stage-two symptoms indicate involvement of organs beyond the skin; and stage three represents persistent infection or symptoms.

## Stage One: Localized/Early Infection

Most people concerned about Lyme disease are familiar with its most common symptom: the red "bull's-eye" rash caused by the body's immune response to infection with *B. burgdorferi*. This rash is different from the small, non-expanding red patch at the site of a tick bite that some people experience. The more limited rash is caused by a local reaction to the bite itself, and in the absence of other symptoms is not an indication of Lyme disease.[7]

Called erythema migrans (EM), the bull's-eye rash has been described in medical literature dating back to the nineteenth century.[8] "Erythema" comes from the Greek word for "red"; "migrans" from the Latin word for "migratory." Seventy-five to 85 percent of people with Lyme disease exhibit this symptom. Rarely, EM may also result from the bite of ticks that do not carry Lyme disease.[9]

In Lyme disease, EM typically takes seven to fourteen days to appear, but it may manifest in three to thirty days. It spreads slowly, 1 to 2 centimeters a day, is warm to the touch, blanches on pressure, is minimally tender, and, rarely, causes tingling or sensitivity at the site. Left untreated, the average EM is 15 centimeters in diameter,

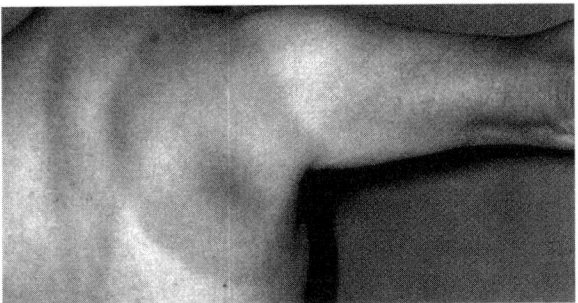

A typical erythema migrans "bull's-eye" rash. Photo by N.Y. Medical College. Centers for Disease Control and Prevention; used with permission.

and may reach 30 centimeters. Secondary EM lesions may occur anyplace on the body in later stages of the disease, but do not usually expand much. At any stage, there may be variations in the shape, texture, and color of the rash.

Although stage one begins with the bite of an infected tick, most people are not aware of the tick or the bite. They realize they might have been infected when the rash appears, or when they have flu-like symptoms (tiredness, stiffness, muscle aches, and joint pains, though without a cough, and usually without gastrointestinal symptoms). The symptoms are occasionally noticed in conjunction with a tick bite. If the disease goes untreated, or is inadequately treated, *B. burgdorferi* "migrate outward in the skin and spread in the lymph or through the blood to other organs or skin sites."[10] The immune systems of some people are apparently able to conquer the disease during stage one: "Among persons infected with *B. burgdorferi* who do not receive antibiotic treatment, 20 [percent] develop only erythema migrans without later manifestations of the disease."[11] However, among those untreated "about 10 to 20 percent . . . will go on to develop chronic arthritis."[12]

## Stage Two: Disseminated Infection

In most people exposed to *B. burgdorferi* through a tick bite, dissemination of the infection to the organs begins "shortly after disease onset, though that dissemination may remain clinically silent for months or even years."[13] During the approximate one-month period of stage two, symptoms include multiple EM lesions, neurological problems, and arthritis. These symptoms may come and go over a number of weeks.

The most common neurological stage-two symptom is Bell's palsy, which is weakness of facial muscles. Heart problems, including heart block and irregular heartbeat,

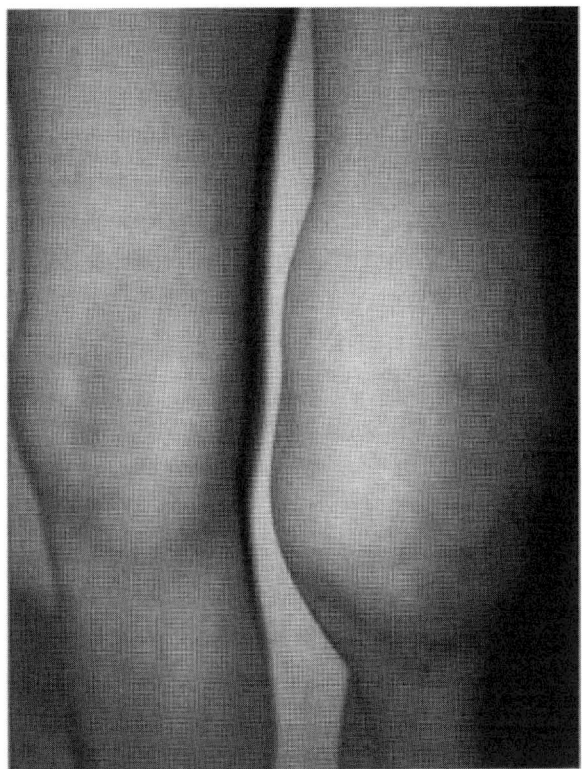

Swollen knee of a youth with Lyme arthritis. National Institutes of Health; used with permission.

are not common but occur at this stage. Stage-two arthritis symptoms most commonly manifest in the large joints, particularly one knee. Such pain is "generally migratory . . . lasting only hours or days in a given location." Episodes at this stage usually involve nondestructive inflammation that "tends to remit without antibiotic treatment . . . but without eradication of the infection."[14]

## Stage Three: Late/Chronic/Persistent Infection (Post–Lyme Disease Syndrome, PLDS)

Patients are generally considered to have late-stage or chronic Lyme disease when they have experienced specific symptoms lasting more than one year. The diagnosis may be made when symptoms had been absent or nearly so and then resurfaced, though most patients experience ongoing symptoms. The symptoms of stage-three infection are usually limited to neurological problems and arthritis.

Sometimes called chronic neuroborreliosis, neurological problems in late-stage Lyme disease manifest as a "subtle encephalopathy [inflammation of the brain] affecting memory, mood, or sleep," and can include spinal pain.[15] Other neurological symptoms manifest as neuropathy, which means problems with sensation or movement. A recent study indicates that "children who had the symptoms of Lyme disease and now have attention and mood problems may be suffering from chronic Lyme disease."[16] Following untreated infection, nervous system abnormalities can develop in several weeks, months, or even years, and the symptoms may linger for weeks or months and may come and go.

Chronic Lyme arthritis is more common than neuroborreliosis, and manifests as pain and swelling in large joints, especially in one knee or the other. Current recommended treatment is for relief of symptoms only. Fortunately, symptoms rarely last more than a few years.

The symptoms of chronic Lyme disease are similar to those of other disorders including chronic fatigue syndrome, which is caused by a virus, and fibromyalgia, inflammation of the body's connective tissues. The significance of the similarities is uncertain, and "there is much debate regarding the relationship" between fibromyalgia and Lyme disease; it is possible that they are wholly separate, but it is also possible that fibromyalgia may be a "sequela [aftereffect] to Lyme disease and that Lyme disease may trigger that disorder."

## Diagnosing Lyme Disease

When it comes to diagnosing Lyme disease, physicians rely on the art as much as the science of medicine. Although testing methods for the disease have improved, Lyme disease is often diagnosed through clinical symptoms. The clinical picture includes, but is not limited to, the presence of the erythema migrans rash, and other symptoms noted in the table on page 41. The onset of symptoms in relation to tick season might also be considered, and the possibility of other diseases whose symptoms are similar to those of Lyme disease should be considered.

Currently, there are three serologic (blood) tests used to diagnose Lyme disease. None detects the actual presence of the germ; rather, as is common in such tests, they look for the presence of antibodies to the germ, because the *B. burgdorferi* microbe "is difficult to isolate or culture from body tissues or fluids."[17] Two of the tests, ELISA and PreVue, are preliminary to the third. ELISA (enzyme-linked immunosorbent assay), the only Lyme antibody test available until recently, must be sent to a laboratory for results. PreVue, a test similar to ELISA, was approved by the Food and Drug Administration in 1999. It can be performed in a doctor's office, and results are available in one hour.[18]

An antibody detection test is usually the first step toward diagnosing or confirming Lyme disease, although it is not useful until two to six weeks after infection because that is how long it usually takes for *B. burgdorferi* antibodies to show up in the blood. If the test is given more than several weeks after infection and the results are negative, the patient might be considered not to have *B. burgdorferi* antibodies, although a second test may be warranted. If a test is negative but clear symptoms of Lyme disease are present, it is usual and appropriate for a doctor to offer treatment anyway so that the patient can benefit from early treatment.

If an ELISA or PreVue test is positive, a second, different test must be performed to confirm the result. ELISA or PreVue may indicate the presence of disease when there is none, or it may indicate the presence of antibodies to germs other than *B. burgdorferi*.[19] The second test, the Western blot, detects antibodies specific to *B. burgdorferi* and reduces the number of false positives obtained with ELISA and PreVue.[20]

Testing for *B. burgdorferi* antibodies, especially in later stages, is further complicated because "[p]atients with previous Lyme disease, particularly if the disease progressed to late stages, often remain seropositive for years, even after adequate antibiotic treatment."[21] And patients who have received the Lyme disease vaccine, LYMErix, may also test positive to ELISA. Data indicates, however, that the Western blot test can detect active infection in recipients of the vaccine.[22]

Clearly there is need for a more definitive test for the presence of active Lyme disease. Ideally, the test would look not for the presence of antibodies, but for the presence of *B. burgdorferi*. In fact, *B. burgdorferi* can be cultured from EM skin scrapings, but such cultures are difficult to accomplish in the laboratory. Similarly, a test called PCR (Polymerase chain reaction) has successfully identified *B. burgdorferi* DNA in cultures from human tissue, but such culture is difficult, and the PCR has not been standardized for routine diagnosis of Lyme disease. PCR can be used to determine if a tick has *B. burgdorferi*, but the information is not helpful with diagnosis of the disease in a person because the tick, even though infected, might not have been attached to the human host long enough to transmit the disease.

Another approach to testing for active Lyme disease seeks to identify *B. burgdorferi* immune complexes (responses of the immune system) "as an adjunctive test to support or exclude *B. burgdorferi* infection." This test was still being developed at the time this book was researched, but preliminary reports indicate potential for such a test.[23] Tests for Lyme disease "that use urine or other body fluids have not been cleared by the FDA."[24]

Until more definitive laboratory testing is available, physicians will have to continue to make their Lyme disease diagnoses based on clinical evidence, sometimes supported by blood tests. This means they will have to walk the fine line between overdiagnosing and underdiagnosing Lyme disease.

Overdiagnosing Lyme disease leads to treatment based on tick bites but without the presence of symptoms. Data indicate that more than 95 percent of bites by blacklegged ticks "do not result in transmission of Lyme disease."[25] Because infection in nymphal ticks, the ones most likely to bite humans, can be as high as 25 to 30 percent, factors other than the bite alone are probably involved in disease transmission.[26] Because an erythema migrans rash can be caused by diseases other than Lyme disease, other diagnoses should be considered for patients who present with the rash but do not live in and have not traveled to a Lyme-endemic area.

Underdiagnosing Lyme disease can have devastating effects on patients, as delay in treatment gives the crafty spirochete *B. burgdorferi* time to wiggle its way into the deep regions of the body, making it less accessible to the body's own immune system and to antibiotics.

It is clear that, next to prevention, early diagnosis is critical to successful treatment of Lyme disease. Toward that end, it is important to seek out a doctor or clinic experienced with Lyme disease diagnosis and treatment. One Lyme disease sufferer, interviewed in an FDA press release, says he "can't emphasize strongly enough the importance of finding a doctor who is experienced in recognizing this infection. As in my case, where Lyme disease is concerned, time is of the essence."[27]

## Treatment

Once the decision to treat a patient for Lyme disease has been made, the initial choice for treatment is an easy one: Antibiotics kill *B. burgdorferi*. In fact, the conclusion early in the mid-twentieth century that erythema migrans, now called Lyme disease, was caused by a bacterium was drawn from evidence that penicillin sometimes cured symptoms.

Many antibiotics work against *B. burgdorferi*, but some work better than others under certain circumstances. Therefore, the antibiotic prescribed depends on the stage of the disease, symptoms exhibited, and the age of the patient. Adjustments are also made for pregnancy. In early-stage infection, oral antibiotics usually do the job; for disseminated and late infection, intravenous antibiotics may be required. In some circumstances, antibiotics may be administered for one to two months, and sometimes longer.

As with other aspects of Lyme disease, that which appears simple on the surface soon becomes complicated. Many questions about the infection remain unanswered, and the answers may affect the way treatment is handled. Researchers do not know, for instance, if symptoms of late or chronic Lyme disease result from *B. burgdorferi* that has lain dormant in the body, or from an autoimmune response in the body, where the body's immune system continues to fight a battle long after the enemy is dead. If the germ remains present, the continued administration of antibiotics might be warranted. If the disease is autoimmune, treatment with anti-inflammatories would be appropriate, but antibiotics would not. Researchers also do not know why some patients treated with antibiotics recover readily from Lyme disease while others, though a small percentage, proceed into the late-infection stage. It is possible that symptoms that do not respond to adequate antibiotic therapy are caused not by Lyme disease, but by another disease with related symptoms.

These uncertainties make treatment choices in the second and third stages of Lyme disease difficult. This difficulty is further compounded by the profound impact that chronic symptoms have on some patients, and by the fact that chronic Lyme disease symptoms are often the same as symptoms for chronic fatigue syndrome and fibromyalgia. For doctors and their patients, finding a proper course of treatment can be frustrating. This frustration is exacerbated by the knowledge that prolonged arthritis symptoms can result in permanent damage to the joints.

In spite of the threat of long-term problems, most patients treated for Lyme disease recover fully, though they may suffer a lingering malaise for months after successful antibiotic treatment. Those who continue to suffer recurrences and long-term symptoms can perhaps best serve themselves by being proactive in their diagnosis and treatment. They can keep up with rapidly occurring advances in knowledge of Lyme disease and its treatment, and connect with others who suffer from Lyme disease by contacting Lyme disease organizations, including those that offer support groups. The names of these organizations are available from health services, from the Centers for Disease Control and Prevention, and by searching the Internet.

Uncertain knowledge about the process of Lyme disease contributes to uncertainty not only for patients, but also for medical systems. Physicians have been investigated by their professional organizations for prescribing prolonged antibiotic treatment of Lyme disease symptoms not recommended as standard protocol. It is perhaps important for those interested in Lyme disease to become knowledgeable about these issues and their outcomes. Current information can be obtained with the assistance of public libraries and through Internet research.

## The Future

Most of the uncertainties about Lyme disease derive from the many questions that remain unanswered:

- How does the organism evade immunological destruction?

- What is the mechanism of chronic neurologic and joint disease?

- What is the full spectrum of late-disease manifestations, and what is the optimal treatment of these manifestations?

- Does the illness ever become self-perpetuating?

- Does spontaneous resolution of clinical manifestation reflect cure or latency?

- What characteristics of the organism and host determine the course of the disease?

In spite of these uncertainties, there is good reason for optimism about the ability to address the disease in the future. Professional and scientific groups, such as the American College of Physicians–Internal Medicine, continue to gather information and provide support to physicians and the public. The National Institutes of Health and other organizations are conducting ongoing research into major Lyme disease problems, including laboratory diagnosis and antibiotic treatment.

Such research will not only help victims of Lyme disease, but the advancements are likely to contribute to understanding other diseases, including emerging infections such as HIV and the hantavirus, and known diseases such as babesiosis and human ganulocytic ehrlichiosis, both of which are transmitted by tick bite, and can be transmitted to humans along with *B. burgdorferi*. These diseases are discussed in Chapter 5.

## Ongoing Efforts Against Lyme Disease

- The National Institutes of Health funded a major study of post–Lyme disease syndrome (chronic Lyme disease). The study was "conducted to determine if treatment for a long period of time, with the antibiotic drugs ceftriaxone and doxycycline, helps patients with chronic Lyme disease." Participating hospitals were New England Medical Center in Boston, Massachusetts; New York Medical College in Valhalla, New York; and Yale University School of Medicine in New Haven, Connecticut.[28] A November 2000 interim review of the study determined that long-term antibiotic treatment does not predictably improve the health or well-being of persons with Lyme disease, and the treatment component of the study was terminated. The studies did not determine whether symptoms of post-treatment chronic Lyme disease (PTCLD) derive from continuing infection or from other causes (www.nih.gov). However, the complete genome for *Borrelia burgdorferi* has been sequenced by scientists at the Institute for Genomic Research (J. Craig Venter Institute). This knowledge is being widely applied in ongoing research on Lyme disease.[29]

- Local and regional studies provide information that contributes to the overall picture of deer tick distribution. For example, a 2000 study at Bemidji State University, Bemidji, Minnesota, reported that *I. scapularous* is present in eight new counties in northern and central Minnesota.[30]

- A number of studies are under way to develop methods for controlling Lyme disease by controlling tick populations:

  1. The *Arthritis Sourcebook* reports that scientists are "pursuing biological control of deer ticks by introducing tiny stingerless wasps, which feed on immature ticks, into tick-infested areas."[31]

  2. The United States Department of Agriculture Agricultural Research Service in Beltsville, Maryland, has tested certain nematodes for "their ability to control adult deer ticks." The nematodes enter "the tick's body, then release their microbial partners," which kill the tick within twenty-four hours. Parasitologist Dolores Hill hopes that the nematodes can reduce the number of egg-laying ticks and thus reduce the overall tick population. Another USDA project explores "the use of fungi as yet another biological alternative to tick-killing chemical sprays."[32]

- The Agricultural Research Service in Kerrville, Texas, is testing tick collars for deer that would kill ticks on the deer. Because blacklegged ticks mate on deer, reducing ticks on deer could reduce the tick population. "The new collaring unit . . . lures deer to a specially designed feeder. To eat, an animal must place its neck near the collaring mechanism, which releases a flexible, self-adjusting collar similar to flea collars worn by cats and dogs . . . Further research, along with a cooperative research and development agree-

## Symptoms and Stages of Lyme Disease*

| Stage | Onset of Symptoms After Infection | Most Common Symptoms |
|---|---|---|
| Stage one: early infection— localized | Days to weeks | • EM rash (erythema migrans)<br>• Muscle and joint aches<br>• Headache<br>• Fever<br>• Fatigue<br>• Chills |
| Stage two: early infection— disseminated | Days to months | • Multiple EM lesions<br>• Meningitis<br>• Radiculitis (numbness, tingling, burning)<br>• Brief episodes of joint pain and swelling, especially in the knee<br>• Facial paralysis (Bell's palsy) |
| Stage three: late infection— persistent | Months to years | • Arthritis, intermittent or chronic<br>• Encephalopathy (mild to moderate confusion) |

**Less Common Symptoms**

- Heart abnormalities
- Eye problems such as conjunctivitis
- Chronic skin disorders
- Encephalomyelitis (limb weakness, poor motor coordination)

Lyme disease is rarely, if ever, fatal.
Having Lyme disease once might not offer immunity against future infection.

*Centers for Disease Control and Prevention; National Institutes of Health

---

ment with Wildlife Management Technologies of Noank, Connecticut, should lead to refinements of this tick-control method."[33]

- *Current Veterinary Therapy* reports that a "Boston-based company, Eco Health, Inc., has developed biodegradable tubes containing permethrin-treated cotton batting that can be placed in infested areas."[34] Mice find the cotton and use it in their nests, where it kills larval and nymphal ticks. The efficacy of this product is not yet verified.[35]

*Lyme on the Web*

There is a great deal of information about Lyme disease on the Internet. Because site addresses often change, you might need to conduct a word search for the following organizations. A general search for "Lyme disease" will also give you new and updated listings. Some sites provide links to other sites.

Remember, anyone can put up a Web site. If you are going to act on information you find online, it is wise to check the credentials of the site. Look for professional credentials and affiliations. Nonprofit and independent organizations should list a board of directors and a street address.

Centers for Disease Control and Prevention
www.cdc.gov

National Institutes of Health
www.nih.gov

Arthritis Foundation
www.arthritis.org

Mayo Clinic
www.mayoclinic.com

World Health Organization
www.who.int

LymeNet
www.lymenet.org

American Lyme Disease Foundation
www.aldf.com

*Chapter 4*
# Preventing Lyme Disease

Prevention is the best medicine for Lyme disease and other tick-borne illnesses. While the task of prevention might seem onerous, it is actually not too difficult to accomplish. It requires a little knowledge, patience, and diligence. The following is a brief discussion of basic prevention techniques, which are explained in detail later in the chapter.

## Lyme Disease Prevention Techniques
### Know Your Habitat

Whether you are at home or traveling, check with local health or natural resources officials to find out if Lyme disease is a problem in the area. If it is, avoid infected

**Reported Cases of Lyme Disease by Year, United States, 1991-2005**

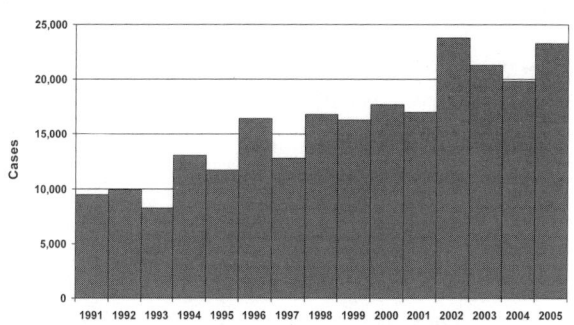

In 2005, 23,305 cases of Lyme disease were reported yielding a national average of 7.9 cases for every 100,000 persons. In the ten states where Lyme disease is most common, the average was 31.6 cases for every 100,000 persons.

Centers for Disease Control and Prevention; used with permission.

**Incidence\* of Lyme Disease, by county of residence, United States, 2002**

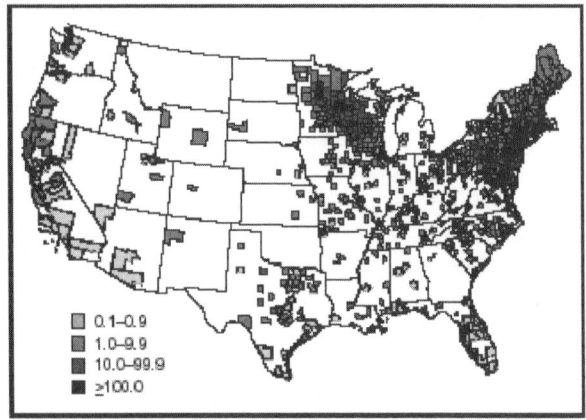

0.1–0.9
1.0–9.9
10.0–99.9
≥100.0

\* Per 100,000 population.

*Note:* This map demonstrates an approximate distribution of predicted Lyme disease risk in the United States. The true relative risk in any given county compared with other counties might differ from that shown here and might change from year to year. Information on risk distribution within states and counties is best obtained from state and local public health authorities. Centers for Disease Control and Prevention; used with permission.

areas or take precautions. If it is not, and you will be in or around wooded areas, still take precautions, and be aware of symptoms of Lyme disease.

## Be Aware of the Seasons

Blacklegged tick nymphs usually take their blood meal from late May through early July; western blacklegged tick nymphs from March through June. Adults usually feed in the fall, but sometimes in the early spring. Larvae take their blood meal in the spring but are not able to transmit infection.

## Wear Appropriate Clothing and Stick to the Beaten Path

If you will be walking in the woods where blacklegged ticks are known to be present, wear light-colored long pants tucked into white socks. Blacklegged tick nymphs, the stage most likely to bite humans, stay close to the ground. Clothing helps keep them off the skin; the light color helps you spot them if they get on the clothes. While out in woods or brushy areas, try to stay on cleared and open paths. If you are in a Lyme-endemic area, remove clothes before entering the house, wash and dry them at high temperatures, and check your body for ticks.

Woodland and forest recreation should not be forgone out of fear of getting Lyme disease. Studies indicate an infection rate of less than 2 percent for persons with identified blacklegged tick bites.[1]

## Use Tick Repellents

Some mosquito repellents applied to the skin also repel ticks. Check the label on the product. A June 2000 *Consumer Reports* article states that HourGuard 12 repelled blacklegged ticks for about nine hours, and Off! Deep Woods for about four hours. They also reported that Repel Permanone, applied to clothing, repelled ticks for two weeks. Repel Permanone must not be used directly on skin. The article "Buzz Off!" includes a brand name listing of repellent features and effectiveness.[2]

Treating limited residential areas with tick pesticides has proven effective, but raises serious environmental and other concerns, including leaching of the chemicals into ground water, and toxic effects on humans and other living creatures. Tick collars intended for animals are toxic to humans. The pesticide on them can be absorbed, and can cause skin lesions. They are not approved by the FDA for human use.

### Clean Up Your Yard

If you live in a tick-endemic area, it can pay to make that area inhospitable to the hosts of blacklegged ticks. Remove or move away woodpiles and other places where mice might flourish. Discourage or prevent deer from entering your yard. Keep the grass mowed and clear shaded areas, opening them to light: Blacklegged ticks like moist, shady areas. And while they can crawl, they don't move very far except via host transport, so cleaning up the yard can help prevent exposure.

### Check for Ticks

Although they are small, blacklegged ticks are not invisible. If you have been out and about in tick country, check your body—or have someone else check it—for roaming or attached ticks. Attached ticks do not wash off in a shower or bath.

### Removing Ticks Not Attached to Your Body

Ticks that are not attached may be removed with your fingers. Do not, however, crush the ticks or break them apart with your fingernails. Doing so releases microscopic germs, including *B. burgdorferi*. Dispose of ticks by burning them or taping them to a piece of paper. Perhaps the best way to dispose of a tick is to put it in alcohol. Many people in tick country keep handy a half-pint jar of rubbing alcohol and drop ticks into it. They keep it closed with a screw-top lid. At season's end, the jar may be emptied outside, or into a toilet. This method has the added benefit of preserving ticks should proper identification become important.

### Remove Attached Ticks Immediately upon Discovery

The causative agent of Lyme disease, *B. burgdorferi,* resides in the gut of blacklegged ticks. The germ is mostly inactive until the tick takes a blood meal. The warm blood nourishes the germ; it begins replicating and migrates from the tick's gut to its mouthparts. This action takes about twenty-four to thirty-six hours. Blacklegged ticks removed within that time are not likely to have transmitted Lyme disease. Still, it is important to watch for Lyme disease symptoms.

### Removing Attached Ticks from Your Body

Remove using tweezers. Do not grab or squeeze the tick with your fingers, as you may inject fluid from the tick into your body, and you don't want to do that. Using the tweezers, grasp the tick as close to the skin as possible. Slowly pull it out. Do not kill the tick by squashing it or breaking it with your fingernails—both actions can release germs from the tick. Dispose of the tick in the trash, burn it, or put it in your alcohol-filled tick jar. Cleanse the site of the bite with soap and water or treat with an antiseptic.

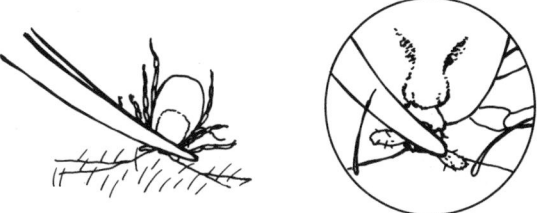

Remove a tick by grasping close to the skin with a tweezers and pulling out slowly but firmly.

Do not remove ticks by any method except by using tweezers. Blacklegged ticks secrete a cement that attaches them to the body. Applying a flame, petroleum jelly, fingernail polish, or other substances will not cause a tick to "back out" of your skin. Applying heat to the tick may cause it to burst, releasing pathogens into the air, and may cause the tick to salivate and expel pathogens into your body.

Attached ticks that are engorged should be handled only while wearing protective gloves or another barrier. These ticks should be saved (in alcohol) for identification, should Lyme disease or other symptoms develop.

Some mouthparts might be left in your skin. Remove them if you can, using tweezers or by manipulating the skin with your fingers; excision is not necessary. Then, wash the area with soap and water. It might be beneficial to apply a topical antibiotic to the area.

## Respond Promptly if You Experience Lyme Disease Symptoms

Lyme disease in the first stage responds quickly to antibiotic treatment. The sooner a diagnosis is made and treatment is started, the less likely that disseminated or chronic Lyme disease will develop. If you do not live in a Lyme-endemic area but have visited one and have Lyme disease symptoms, tell your doctor. Refer to Chapter 3 for further discussion of symptoms and treatments.

## Research on Lyme Disease Vaccines

In 2002, citing poor sales, the pharmaceutical company GlaxoSmithKline discontinued production of LYMErix, a vaccine for Lyme disease approved in 1998 by the FDA. The vaccine had become controversial when use of it was linked to the onset of arthritis. The National Institutes of Health report that in addition to seeking new vaccines for humans, scientists hope to treat Lyme disease in mice. Early results of trials indicate that delivering the vaccine to mice in the field in endemic areas could disrupt transmission of Lyme disease (*Vaccine*, 24; 1949, 2006).[3]

## Especially for Children

Children who play outside in Lyme-endemic areas should be protected from tick bites. They should be checked for ticks at the end of the day, with the help of adults or siblings. Ticks removed within twenty-four hours of attachment have not usually had time to transmit the disease.

If children will be walking in brushy or grassy areas, they should wear suitable light-colored clothing, and trousers should be tucked into socks. In addition, masking tape can be used to close the gap between the trousers and socks. A final layer of tape can be placed sticky side out to catch climbing ticks.

Keeping play areas clear of brush, woodpiles, and other favorable tick habitats can also help protect children. Statistics indicate that children have fewer tick bites playing in front yards, away from backyards that are bordered by woods.[4]

Outside recreation is important for everyone, especially for children, and it is not necessary for children to stay inside to avoid Lyme disease. Preventative measures can be taken, and should symptoms occur, prompt treatment is almost always successful.

*Summary of Preventative Measures\**

- Learn about blacklegged ticks and Lyme disease in areas where you live or visit.

- Wear light-colored clothing and tuck long pants into socks.

- Use tick repellents.

- Remove attached ticks promptly and carefully, using tweezers (so you don't inject tick fluids into your body).

- Know Lyme disease symptoms and immediately seek medical help if they appear.

- If you live in a Lyme-endemic area, make your yard inhospitable to blacklegged ticks by minimizing the presence of their hosts: discourage mice by clearing out woodpiles and brushy areas; exclude deer; open shaded areas to light.

\*Adapted in part from "Lyme Disease," Minnesota Department of Health.

# Chapter 5

# Other U.S. Tick-Borne Diseases

Ticks are bad news. They are excellent hosts to all kinds of germs—bacteria, viruses, parasites—and in some cases their bites alone are toxic. They come in two forms, hard-shell and soft-shell. The hard-shell ticks, such as blacklegged ticks, the cause of Lyme disease, at least give humans a chance: It normally takes twenty-four hours of attachment before a germ can migrate to the tick's mouth-parts and into your skin, so you have opportunity to find and remove them before they transmit disease. However, some soft-shell ticks, such as *Ornithodoros hermsi*, which transmits relapsing fever, can satisfy their needs in less than one hour.[1] They're filled up and gone before we can notice them on our skin, often leaving their hitchhiking, disease-causing germs safely inoculated into our bodies.

Lyme disease is the number one tick-borne illness in the United States, with more than 15,000 cases reported annually to the Centers for Disease Control.[2] Although it is a serious disease, it is rarely, if ever, fatal.[3] Because Lyme disease is an emerging infection, our knowledge of it and its complications is also emerging, and it is possible symptoms of other tick-borne illnesses, as well as non-tick-borne diseases (such as fibromyalgia and chronic fatigue syndrome) can be confused with the symptoms of Lyme disease. It is also possible that more than one tick-borne disease can strike a person at the same time. In fact, babesiosis and ehrlichiosis, described in this chapter, are carried by the blacklegged ticks that carry Lyme disease, and can be cotransmitted.[4]

The process of making an accurate diagnosis for tick-borne and other illnesses is complicated. It includes evaluation of symptoms and serology (blood work), and brings geographic locations and seasons into consideration, among other factors. It is important for persons with symptoms of, or related to, tick-borne illnesses to seek immediate medical help. Treatment can prevent progression of disease, and with some diseases can be lifesaving. Persons with persistent, confusing symptoms and questionable diagnosis can perhaps find relief or comfort—or both—by consulting with medical experts in the field of tick-borne illnesses.

Taking preventative measures against the bites of blacklegged ticks, as described in Chapter 2, also are effective against the bites of other ticks.

| **Common Names of Tick Vectors** | |
|---|---|
| *Ixodes scapularis* | Blacklegged tick |
| *Ixodes pacificus* | Western blacklegged tick |
| *Dermacentor variabilis* | Dog tick, wood tick |
| *Dermacentor andersoni* | Rocky Mountain wood tick |
| *Amblyomma americanum* | Lone Star tick |
| *Ornithodoros* species | Soft ticks including *O. hermsi* and *O. turicata* (relapsing fever tick) in the U.S. |

## Rocky Mountain Spotted Fever

Prior to the identification of Lyme disease, Rocky Mountain spotted fever was probably the most commonly recognized tick-borne illness in the United States. It gained notoriety in the second half of the nineteenth century in Montana. Settlers were beset by the disease, which is sometimes fatal. Following efforts by the Montana Board of Health in the late 1800s, Dr. Howard Taylor Ricketts discovered in the early 1900s that the disease is caused by a bacterium, which was later named for him, *Rickettsia rickettsii.*[5]

Rocky Mountain spotted fever is transmitted by *Dermacentor andersoni,* the Rocky Mountain wood tick, and *D. variabilis,* the dog tick. Left: *Dermacentor andersoni,* adult female.

In spite of its common name, Rocky Mountain spotted fever is primarily a disease of the southeast and west south-central United States. More than 400 cases were reported to the National Institutes of Health in 1994. The disease commonly provokes multiple symptoms such as fever, headache, and rash. Other symptoms include abdominal pain, confusion, and organ failure and dysfunction. The disease is especially common on the Atlantic seacoast and occurs mostly from May to September, when people and ticks are active outdoors.

Ticks carrying Rocky Mountain fever must usually be attached to a human for six to ten hours for disease transmission to occur. The disease in humans can be detected by an antibody test, but the National Institutes of Health stress that treatment must begin before test results are in. Prompt treatment has led to a reduction in mortality from 25 to 5 percent. Even with appropriate treatment, full recovery may take months. Survivors reap one benefit: lifelong immunity to the disease.

## Babesiosis

Babesiosis is one of two recently detected diseases that are often described in literature on Lyme disease. Babesiosis is carried by both blacklegged ticks and western black-legged ticks, the vectors that carry the Lyme disease germ.

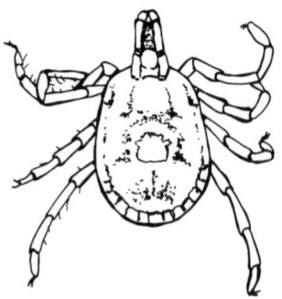

Babesiosis is transmitted by *Amblyomma americanum,* the Lone Star tick; *D. variabilis,* the dog tick; and *I. scapularis,* the eastern blacklegged tick. Right: *Amblyomma americanum,* adult female.

Babesiosis can be transmitted with Lyme disease during a tick bite, and its symptoms can be misdiagnosed as Lyme disease symptoms. Severity and duration of symptoms "greater than normal" have been associated with codiagnosis of babesiosis and Lyme disease.

Babesiosis is caused by a parasite that infects red blood cells. Although it can be confused with Lyme disease, it is more closely related to malaria, another parasite. The incidence of babesiosis is unknown, because many people have no symptoms, which include fever and anemia. It most commonly occurs in the Northeast during the summer months. It is diagnosed with laboratory tests; the National Institutes of Health reported that more than 450 cases had been reported since the disease appeared in 1968. An antiparasitic drug is used to treat babesiosis, but even without treatment the disease usually resolves on its own. It is rarely fatal.

## Ehrlichiosis
### Human Monocytic Ehrlichiosis (HME); Human Granulocytic Ehrlichiosis (HGE)

Like babesiosis, the two identified forms of ehrlichiosis can be cotransmitted with Lyme disease, or transmitted independently. The diseases are caused by a rickettsial bacterium; their symptoms are similar and include fever, chills, headaches, and vomiting. Symptoms are especially confused with those of Rocky Mountain spotted fever. Ehrlichiosis is transmitted by *Amblyomma americanum*, the lone star tick, *D. variabilis*, the dog tick, and *I. scapularis*, the blacklegged tick.

Because ehrlichiosis is so newly identified (1987), specific diagnostic tests have yet to be developed. Diagnosis is therefore made on evaluation of symptoms and of related laboratory findings such as those on organ functions. The CDC receives reports on an average of fifty cases per year.[6] For both forms, most people treated with antibiotics recover completely; however, complications can arise, especially in older people and those who do not receive quick treatment. The mortality rate for both forms of the disease may be as high as 5 percent.[7]

## Relapsing Fever (Tick Fever, Recurrent Fever, Famine Fever)

Relapsing fever is caused by the spirochete *Borrelia hermsii*, which is in the same genus as the Lyme disease bacterium. *B. hermsii* is carried by lice and ticks. Currently, louse-borne relapsing fever is limited to parts of northern and central Africa, but in "past decades [it] caused millions of cases of disease in people, including many in the United States and Europe." The last relapsing fever epidemic followed World War II and took place in the Middle East and North Africa.[8]

Today relapsing fever is uncommon in the United States. It is "the only disease transmitted by the soft-body tick, *Ornithodoros*, found mainly in remote mountainous settings." This description of a setting for disease transmission should encourage anyone with a seasonal home

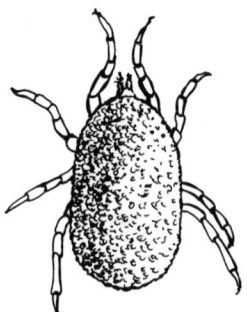

Relapsing fever is caused by *Ornithodoros* species ticks, especially *O. hermsi*. Right: *O. hermsi,* adult female.

to keep it clean and rodent-free: Human cases of illness tend to peak in the warmer months, since when it's too cold, the ticks can't move. But the disease can occur year-round. A common scenario for human infection is to have a tick population established with rodents [including chipmunks and squirrels] who've made their home in rustic mountain cabins . . . in attics, walls, basements, or under the floor. "If the rodents die off, leave, or hibernate, the ticks look for other hosts. In winter, people often will stay in these cabins and warm them up for a week. The rodents are not active, the ticks get warmed up, and they become hungry and start moving around looking for a food source. A person who's breathing is basically a carbon dioxide generator. The ticks actually orient to a carbon dioxide gradient, and this is one of the ways they find their hosts."

Unlike the leisurely hard-body tick, soft-body ticks take their meals in as little as ten to ninety minutes. The bite is painless, and may go undetected. Symptoms usually occur within seven days and include a scab at the bite site, fever, chills, and muscle and joint pain. The disease earns its name, relapsing fever, because if left untreated symptoms wane and then recur, usually three to five times before the disease resolves.

Relapsing fever is diagnosed with laboratory tests. The presence of the relapsing fever bacterium can cause a false positive test for Lyme disease, but the diseases can be distinguished using the Western blot test. Treatment is with antibiotics. Even without treatment, death is rare.

## Colorado Tick Fever (Mountain Fever)

This disease is caused by a virus, and 200 to 300 cases are reported annually in the United States. It is transmitted by *D. andersoni,* the Rocky Mountain wood tick, and is limited primarily to mountainous western states. Symptoms, which include fever, chills, nausea, and muscle aches, may wane and then recur one time. The disease is diagnosed with laboratory tests. Because it is a virus, no treatment is available, but symptoms can be relieved with medication. Fatalities are rare. Because the disease can be transmitted by blood transfusions, a person who has had the disease should not donate blood for at least six months. An episode of the disease provides long-lasting immunity to future infection.

## Tularemia (Rabbit Fever, Deerfly Fever)

Most people have heard of tularemia in relation to handling diseased rabbits, and that is one way to contract it. However, more than half the cases are caused by tick bites.

Tularemia occurs in two forms, one mild and one more severe. Symptoms of both forms include swollen lymph glands and a sore at the bite site. "The disease may be mild and self-limited, with fever abating in 4 weeks. A more fulminant disease leads to fever with chills, headache, abdominal pain, and severe prostration." Diagnosis is made based on symptoms, but may be confirmed with

**Major Tick-Borne Diseases and Vectors in the United States**

| Disease | Organism | Principal Vectors | Region |
|---|---|---|---|
| Lyme disease | *Borrelia burgdorferi* | *Ixodes scapularis*<br>(*I. dammini*)<br>(*I. pacificus*) | Northeast, Midwest,<br>Mid-Atlantic<br>West Coast |
| Rocky Mountain spotted fever | *Rickettsia rickettsii* | *Dermacentor variabilis*<br>*D. andersoni* | East, South<br>West |
| Babesiosis | *Babesia microti*<br>*B. equi* | *I. scapularis*<br>*I. pacificus* | Northeast<br>West Coast |
| Ehrlichiosis or human monocytic ehrlichiosis (HME)† | *Ehrlichia chaffeensis* | *D. variabilis*<br>*Amblyomma americanum*<br>*I. scapularis* | South-Atlantic<br>South-Central |
| Human granulocytic ehrlichiosis (HGE)† | *E. equi* | *I. scapularis*<br>*I. pacificus (?)*<br>*D. variabilis (?)* | Cases have been reported in Minnesota, Wisconsin, California, Florida, Massachusetts, New York |

| | | | |
|---|---|---|---|
| Relapsing fever | *Borrelia hermsii* | *Ornithodoros* species, especially *O. hermsi*‡ | West |
| Colorado tick fever | Coltivirus | *D. andersoni* | West |
| Tularemia | Francisella tularensis | *A. americanum* *D. andersoni* *D. variabilis* | Southeast/South-Central West Widespread |
| Tick paralysis | Toxin (not a bacterium or virus) | *D. andersoni* *D. variabilis* | West East |

†HME was first observed in humans in 1986 and its bacteria was isolated in 1991. HGE was first described in 1994 and the bacterium that causes it was identified in 1996 (NIH). "Because human infections are caused by two genetically different *Ehrlichia* species with distinct serologic reactions, which infect different host cells, the disease caused by *E. chaffeensis* is called human monocytic ehrlichiosis, while that caused by the *E. equi*–like organism is called human granulocytic ehrlichiosis (HGE)" (Edelman, p. 41).
‡Goddard, p. 286

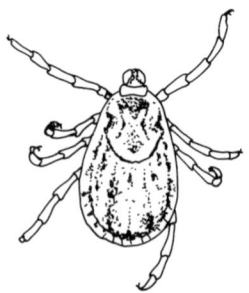

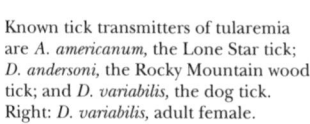

Known tick transmitters of tularemia are *A. americanum,* the Lone Star tick; *D. andersoni,* the Rocky Mountain wood tick; and *D. variabilis,* the dog tick. Right: *D. variabilis,* adult female.

laboratory tests that are successful four to six weeks after onset of the disease. Treatment is with antibiotics and recovery is usually full. Having the disease usually provides long-lasting immunity to it.

## Tick Paralysis

Tick paralysis is a rare disease, and is caused not by infection but by a neurotoxin produced in the tick's salivary gland. Symptoms begin with weakness in both legs and progress to paralysis that then "ascends upward to trunk, arms, and head within hours and may lead to respiratory failure and death." Diagnosis is made by evaluation of symptoms and discovery of an embedded tick. Treatment consists of removal of the tick, which is usually lodged in the scalp, and "results in resolution of symptoms within several hours to days." In cases that go undiagnosed and where the tick is not removed, a mortality rate of 10 to 12 percent is reported.[9] Tick paralysis is transmitted by *D. andersoni,* the Rocky Mountain tick, and by *D. variabilis,* the dog tick.

# Chapter 6

# Ticks International

Ticks abound on our planet, and in general they are vectors for diseases that can be transferred to humans. It is never a good idea to let a tick bite you, even though the bites of some ticks are benign.

As with Lyme disease, most tick-borne illnesses are associated with rodent host reservoirs for the germ or parasite. A germ lives in a host reservoir such as a mouse. A tick feeds on the mouse and acquires the disease, then passes it on to a human during a subsequent feeding.

It is important when traveling abroad, and even when traveling within the United States, to know about health concerns in the areas you visit. If you will be staying in cities or in well-kept tourist accommodations, you need not worry much about tick-borne illnesses. Still, it is a good idea to be aware of diseases endemic to the area, and of their symptoms. If, after leaving the area, you develop symptoms that might be related to a tick bite, seek medical guidance, and bring with you any information you have on illnesses you might have been exposed to.

If, when traveling, you will be hiking, camping, or living in nonurban areas, it is important to find out ahead of time if ticks are indigenous to the area, and what diseases they might transmit. If they are a problem, follow the prevention measures discussed in this chapter and refer to Chapter 4 as well. Be especially aware of symptoms of indigenous diseases, and be prepared to act quickly if you experience those symptoms. If medical help is not readily available and the disease is caused by a bacterium, you might want to consult with a doctor about carrying appropriate antibiotics with you. Because most tick-borne bacterial illnesses require specific antibiotics for successful treatment, it is usually not useful to carry a generic one.

Whether visiting urban or rural areas, it is imperative to insist on healthy living conditions. Lodgings and campsites should be fastidiously clean and rodent-free. Avoidance of ticks is the best preventative measure, and freedom from rodents often implies freedom from ticks. If you will be staying in a lodging, such as a cabin, that has been closed up for some time, insist that it be thoroughly cleaned and purged of rodents. Bedding should be freshly laundered.

Ticks, of course, are not the only vectors for human disease: Other arthropods such as mosquitoes, fleas, flies, and lice transmit illness to humans. Disease is also transmitted through water, and even through the air. In some areas of the world, there are few if any such problems. Other areas may be rife with them. Before traveling, arm yourself with knowledge about diseases you might be exposed to, and follow recommended guidelines for avoiding exposure, including the use of appropriate clothing, repellents, and bed nets. Vaccinations are available to prevent many diseases, and in some cases are required for entry into a country, or for reentry into the United States.

## Preventing Tick-Borne Illness While Traveling Abroad

1. Review and follow the prevention measures discussed in Chapter 4, including use of protective clothing and tick repellents.

2. Check with health authorities to learn about prevention, symptoms, and treatment of indigenous diseases in areas you will visit. You can obtain such information

from embassies, in public libraries, and by searching the Internet, especially public health sites such as the World Health Organization and the Centers for Disease Control and Prevention, and sites maintained by universities with medical schools. Most medical clinics have a designated international medicine specialist. Visit one before you travel.

3. Avoid rodent populations and areas they frequent. Be especially wary of their nests, their droppings, and water contaminated with their droppings. Insist on clean, rodent-free accommodations.

4. Be alert for symptoms of tick-borne diseases, with or without evidence of a tick bite. Prophylactic treatment for a bite alone, in the absence of symptoms of illness, is not usually recommended. It is, however, in some circumstances, especially if a pregnant woman experiences the symptoms. Consult with knowledgeable professionals. Treatment for most tick-borne illnesses is successful if it is begun early in the disease. Antibiotic treatment has greatly reduced the fatality rate for a number of bacterial tick-borne diseases.

5. Health warnings about countries outside of North America, issued by health agencies, generally deal with infectious diseases that are passed from person to person or through water. If you will be hiking, camping, or living in indigenous or wild settings, seek information from knowledgeable professionals about dangers from tick and other bug-transmitted diseases.

## Lyme Disease Abroad

The symptoms of Lyme disease were first recognized in Europe at least as early as the 1900s. The disease associated

## A Sampling of Tick-Borne Illnesses
This sampling is not inclusive. Seek expert advice about tick-borne illnesses in specific locations.

| Disease | Distribution | Symptoms (Not Inclusive) | Causative Agent | Treatment | Outcome |
|---|---|---|---|---|---|
| Australian rickettsial spotted fever (Queensland tick typhus) ("Ticks") | Australia | Symptoms include weakness in limbs; rashes; headache; and fever | Toxin | Removal of tick; antitoxin | "Development of a tick antitoxin and modern medicine have prevented further deaths . . ." |
| Ehrlichiosis (Berkow, p. 894) | Throughout the world | Resembles Rocky Mountain spotted fever, but without the rash | Bacteria | Antibiotics | Untreated, it can be fatal |
| Lyme disease (Centers for Disease Control and Prevention) | "Temperate forested regions of Europe and Asia and in northeastern, north central, and Pacific coastal regions of North America. It is not [known to be] transmitted in the tropics." | Erythema migrans (bull's-eye-shaped) rash; flu-like symptoms; joint pains and aches | Bacteria | Antibiotics | Rarely if ever fatal; treatment with antibiotics usually results in cure; early treatment usually prevents long-term complications |
| Relapsing fever (Aly, p. 879) | North and South America, Africa, Asia, Europe (louseborne transmission is limited to parts of Africa and South America) | Chills; fever; rapid heart rate; headache; joint pain | Bacteria | Antibiotics | Mortality rate is less than 5 percent; treatment with antibiotics cures the disease |

with them was called erythema migrans after the signature bull's-eye rash. The name Lyme disease has been accepted worldwide for infection with the spirochete bacterial species *Borrelia burgdorferi sl* (*sensu lato*, meaning the broader category "species"). Many strains of *B. burgdorferi sl* have been identified, including *B. burgdorferi ss* (*sensu stricto*, meaning a strain within the species of the same name), *B. garinii*, and *B. afzelii*. Only these three strains are, to date, confirmed to cause Lyme disease. The distinctions are important because while all result in the erythema migrans rash in most people infected with them, each is associated, in degree, with different symptoms, as shown in the chart below.

| Variations in Lyme Disease Symptoms by *Borrelia burgdorferi* Strain (EUCALB)* | | | |
|---|---|---|---|
| **Strain of *B. burgdorferi* sl** | **Geographic Location** | **Symptoms Especially Associated with the Strain** | **Tick Vector (Aly, p. 164)** |
| *B. burgdorferi ss* | North America and Europe | Arthritis | *Ixodes scapularis; Ixodes pacificus; Ixodes ricinus* |
| *B. garinii* | Europe, especially western Europe | Neurological symptoms | *Ixodes ricinus* |
| *B. afzelii* | Europe, especially central Europe and Scandinavia | Chronic skin condition | *Ixodes ricinus* |
| *Note: Overlap in most, if not all, symptoms does occur; the erythema migrans rash is common to all. | | | |

Other *Borrelia burgdorferi sl* strains have been identified in the U.S. (*B. lonestari*), Japan, Russia, Asia, and Eurasia, but they are not yet associated with Lyme disease.

The precautions, diagnosis, and treatments that apply to Lyme disease in North America, discussed in earlier chapters, apply to Lyme disease in Europe.

# Chapter 7

# Lyme Disease in Pets and Other Animals

*Borrelia burgdorferi,* the microbe that causes Lyme disease, has been found in ticks and animals all around the world. It has been identified in camels in Africa, rodents in Taiwan, ticks on seabirds within the Arctic and Antarctic Circles, dogs in Australia, ticks in Japan, lizards in California, and in rabbits, cattle, horses, and, of course, deer in the United States and Europe.

It is clear that *B. burgdorferi* is eclectic in its choice of hosts. However, it is still not easy for the germ to move from hosts in the wild to hosts in the human realm. For that to happen, a suitable vector, one that will transmit the germ from one host to another, must be available. To be suitable, the vector must meet two conditions: it must have a significant rate of infection within its population (i.e., many *Ixodes* tick in an area must be infected), and it must be prone to biting humans and their pets and animals.

Currently, these conditions are met in relatively small regions of the globe: limited areas of North America (in the United States the areas include the Northeast, Midwest, and some areas of the West Coast), and in Europe. While the *Ixodes* ticks that transmit Lyme disease are present throughout most of the United States, they are not all suitable vectors for Lyme disease. *Ixodes scapularis* in the South and *Ixodes pacificus* in the West, for instance, tend to take their meals from lizards, and *B. burgdorferi* does not thrive in lizards. Furthermore, on the West Coast, other ticks carry *B. burgdorferi,* but they are ticks that do not bite humans.

With many features of Lyme disease—but not all—that which applies to humans also applies to pets and farm animals. The main, if not the only, source of transmission are the North American ticks *Ixodes scapularis* and *Ixodes pacificus,* and the European tick *Ixodes ricinus.* Treatment is with antibiotics, and is usually successful. Lyme disease cases in animals, as in humans, are usually limited to areas where the disease is established.

There are differences: Animals do not usually exhibit the erythema migrans rash that shows up in about 80 percent of humans afflicted with Lyme disease. Other symptoms of the disease are similar to those seen in humans, but lean more heavily toward arthritis-like symptoms. Animals do not seem to suffer from chronic Lyme disease, as do some humans, and when relapse occurs, it is successfully treated with antibiotics. Treatment with antibiotics is no longer recommended for chronic Lyme disease in humans. Even without treatment, Lyme disease in dogs often resolves on its own.

Another major difference between Lyme disease in dogs and humans is the stage of the tick that most often transmits the disease. Most cases in dogs come from adult ticks; most in humans are from nymphs.

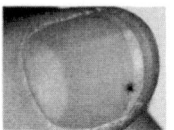
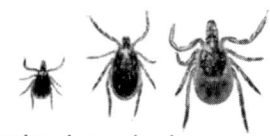

Left: *Ixodes scapularis* nymph as compared to a human thumb.
Right: *Ixodes scapularis* (enlarged)—most common tick vector in northeastern and midwestern United States (from left to right: nymph, adult male, adult female). National Institutes of Health; used with permission.

Among pets and farm animals, dogs seem to be the most vulnerable to Lyme disease. In areas where their owners are at risk, dogs are as well. Cats are able to get Lyme disease, but they rarely do, probably because of their constant grooming and removal of ticks. Because of that very behavior, humans are more likely to be exposed to ticks from cats than they are from dogs. *Ixodes* ticks are heat-seekers, and once on a dog they quickly latch on to feed and stay attached until sated. Cats, on the other hand, are likely to flick off the ticks, which are then free to latch on to a human host in the cat's household.

It appears unlikely that contagious transmission of the Lyme disease germ, from animals to people or animals to animals, can occur. For example, although *B. burgdorferi* has been found in dog urine, "viable organisms deteriorate quickly in urine and saliva, and are virtually impossible to isolate by culture." In addition, there is "no evidence of increased risk among those who own or handle dogs."[1]

To date, among farm animals, only cattle and horses are known to suffer from Lyme disease. Symptoms in cattle include fever, stiffness, swollen joints, and decreased milk production. Symptoms in horses include chronic weight loss, sporadic lameness, low-grade fever, swollen joints, and muscle tenderness. Both animals are usually successfully treated with antibiotics.

## Preventing Lyme Disease in Dogs

With dogs, as with humans, the first line of defense against Lyme disease is protection from exposure to ticks.

1. Learn about avoiding blacklegged ticks in areas where you live or visit.

2. In Lyme-endemic areas, avoid taking pets out into the woods or other areas where ticks are prevalent. This precaution against Lyme disease is not necessary in areas where Lyme disease is not endemic; however, it may be prudent as a means to prevent other tick-

borne illnesses that affect pets, such as tick paralysis.

3. Use preventative measures. To make an appropriate choice for your pet and the area you live in, discuss options and combinations of options with your veterinarian or another reliable source.

- Groom pets frequently, outside, especially after walks in the woods or brushy or grassy areas.

- Use tick collars, which do a good job of protecting pets from tick bites.

- Use medications such as Frontline and Advantix to protect pets from ticks.

- Use preventative dips that contain effective tick repellents.

- A Lyme disease vaccine is available for dogs aged nine weeks or older. (There is no vaccine for cats.) It is usually recommended only in Lyme-endemic areas, and only for dogs at high risk to exposure. Even then, other measures may be as or more effective, and may be safer. Because the vaccine is relatively new, all safety and efficacy questions have not been resolved. Discuss this and other options with your veterinarian.

4. If a tick is found attached to a pet, remove it immediately. It usually takes a minimum of twenty-four hours of attachment for the germ, warmed and energized by the blood meal, to migrate from the tick's gut to its salivary glands and into the tick's host.

5. Remove the tick with care. As with ticks on humans, improper removal may inject blood and microbes into the pet. If the tick is engorged, it is wise to wear gloves or use some skin barrier to protect your skin from exposure to the tick's blood. For proper removal, use

tweezers: Grasp the tick as close to the skin as possible, and slowly, steadily pull it out. Mouthparts left in the skin do not usually cause problems. The area may be swabbed with alcohol and treated with an antibiotic salve, but usually neither is necessary.

6. Be aware of the symptoms of Lyme disease in dogs and immediately seek veterinary care if symptoms appear. Treatment with antibiotics is highly successful. If you live in a nonendemic area but have traveled to one, be sure to tell your veterinarian that your pet could have been exposed to Lyme disease.

7. Be alert to new prevention products and new knowledge about Lyme disease. Research is ongoing, and additional options are likely to become available.

## Symptoms in Dogs

Lyme disease symptoms usually do not manifest in dogs until two to five months after exposure. The dominant symptoms are acute arthritis and lameness. Joints may be swollen and warm. Other symptoms include fever, anorexia, lethargy, and swollen lymph nodes. The chronic arthritis that sometimes results from Lyme disease in humans is rarely seen in dogs.

## Diagnosis of Dogs

As with Lyme disease in humans, Lyme disease symptoms in pets mimic other diseases. Diagnosis therefore is not simple and relies as much on the art as on the science of medicine. It is usually made based on the likelihood of a bite by an infected tick (i.e., with consideration of geographic location and season) and symptoms expressed. The diagnosis can be confirmed with the same laboratory tests used to confirm Lyme disease in humans. The first test, ELISA, may have false positives, which can be verified with the Western blot test. A prompt reduction of symptoms with antibiotic treatment can also be taken as a confirmation of the diagnosis.

As with humans, treatment based solely on evidence of a tick bite is rarely recommended, even in Lyme-endemic areas. However, treatment when symptoms are present should not be delayed while waiting for confirming laboratory tests.

## Treatment of Dogs

Antibiotic treatment of animals with Lyme disease is almost always successful. Treatment is usually longer than for other diseases: twenty-one to twenty-eight days is recommended, in part because of the slow multiplication rate of *B. burgdorferi.*

## Prognosis for Dogs

Dogs usually recover completely from symptoms twenty-four to forty-eight hours after antibiotic treatment is begun. Anti-inflammatories can also be used to treat arthritic symptoms. Occasionally symptoms will reappear. Retreatment with antibiotics is usually successful. Symptoms that occur six months to a year after successful treatment might be due to reexposure to infected ticks, rather than to a recurrence of the disease. The infection apparently does not transfer to the fetuses of pregnant bitches.[2]

## Lyme Disease in Cats

Lyme disease in cats is rare, but when it does occur, symptoms, diagnosis, treatment, and prognosis are similar to those for dogs.

# Chapter 8

# The Cousins: Black Widow and Brown Recluse Spiders, Scorpions, Chiggers, and Scabies

Arthropoda is the largest by far of phyla in the animal kingdom. It claims around 700,000 known species, distinguished primarily by their external skeletons, and often by their segmented appendages. The next closest phylum is Mollusca with around 70,000 known species, including snails, clams, and octopi. Chordata follows close behind with around 60,000 known species, including the human species.

In the United States, ticks are the most significant arthropod vector for disease, but their cousins, including spiders, scorpions, and mites, also affect human health, though they rarely cause death. Spiders and scorpions afflict us with toxins; chigger and scabies mites parasitize us. As with ticks, prevention is the best medicine for conditions caused by these creatures.

## Black Widow Spider

The black widow spider, *Latrodectus mactans,* is one of several "widow" species of spiders in the United States and inhabits every state except Alaska, though it is more common in the South and West. It is a reclusive spider, preferring to hang out in attics and closets and under floorboards. It catches its prey—other spiders and insects—in its web, which has an erratic shape.

Fitting with its reclusive nature, the black widow spider only attacks if provoked. As with other spiders, if its

Female black widow spider, *Latrodectus mactans*, showing hourglass figure on abdomen.

Black widow spider, dorsal (top) view.

mate dies, it might eat it, and it might even kill its mate in order to eat it if other food is not available. However, some male black widows mate with more than one female, and most die of their own accord after mating. Females may live up to three years.

Female and male black widows are shiny black and have the same shape, but differ in important ways. The female, with a 30- to 40-millimeter (about 1.5 inches) leg span, is larger, and has a red hourglass marking on its belly. The male is smaller, with a 16- to 20-millimeter (about 0.75 inch) leg span, and has red and white marks on its belly. More important, the bite of the female is venomous to humans, while the bite of the male is not. It is not clear if the venom of the male is less potent, is present in less quantity, or if the shorter fangs of the male do not inject as much venom with a bite. The bite of an immature female black widow spider is similar to that of a male.

Contrary to popular belief, the bite of a black widow spider is not a death sentence. In fact, death is rare, with a rate estimated from less than 1 percent to 4 to 6 percent.[1] Some people are not even aware they have been bitten; others experience a sharp pinprick, followed by a dull pain in the area around the bite. Bites most typically occur on the hand and foot, although in the past when outhouses were common, the buttocks and genitals were common targets.

When it bites, the black widow injects a toxin into its prey. The usual victim is another arthropod, an insect or spider, which provides food for the black widow. The toxin paralyzes tiny creatures; in humans, it causes a variety of symptoms including severe muscle pain in the abdomen, chest wall, and elsewhere. It can also cause restlessness, anxiety, sweating, headaches, breathing problems, nausea and vomiting, and other reactions.

A black widow spider bite should be treated as a medical emergency. A trip to an urgent care facility or the emergency room is recommended, and is especially warranted if the victim is a child, elderly, or not in good health. If the reaction to the bite is a mild one, it will resolve on its own, but if the reaction is severe, complications can occur. These can usually be prevented with medical treatment, which might include the administration of medications that counteract symptoms caused by the toxin. Antivenin is available, but is used judiciously as it can cause a serious reaction of its own. Hospitalization is recommended for severe cases, and especially for children, the elderly, and those not in good health, including those with heart conditions or high blood pressure.

Follow-up treatment for a black widow spider bite might include use of muscle relaxants to reduce muscle spasms and pain. Hot baths can also be helpful.

## Brown Recluse Spider (Fiddleback Spider)

The brown recluse spider, *Loxosceles reclusa*, is less well known than the black widow and its United States range is more limited, generally from the East Coast westward to Arizona and Wyoming. It is medium-sized, has a 2- to 4-centimeter leg span, is tan or brown with a violin-shaped marking near its head, and sports six eyes. It earns its "recluse" name by preferring to stay out of sight. It likes a dark and undisturbed habitat, such as woodpiles and stor-

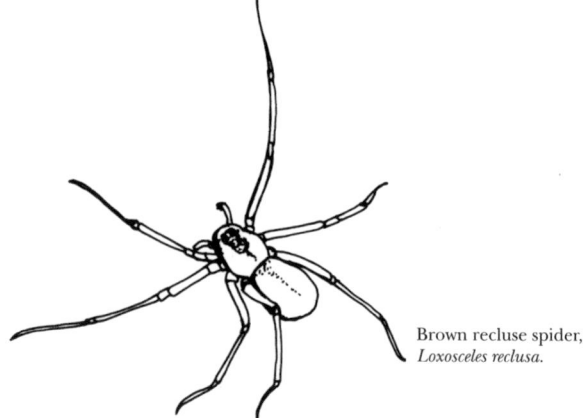

Brown recluse spider,
*Loxosceles reclusa.*

age closets. Most bites occur when a person reaches into the brown recluse's space, or puts on clothing, especially little-used clothing, that the spider is residing in.

The bite of a brown recluse spider may be felt as an intense sting or may be painless. Symptoms may be noticed in three to eight hours, when the bite site becomes red, swollen, and tender. The toxin injected can cause death of the tissue around the bite, and the sore can enlarge and become ulcerous. Healing can be slow, taking six to eight weeks and the lesion can result in a prominent scar. One study indicates that this necrosis (tissue death) occurs in less than half of documented brown recluse bites.

Immediate medical treatment is warranted for a brown recluse spider bite. Although the primary symptom is a rash or deterioration of skin at the site, systemic complications can and do occur, including malaise, nausea, anemia, and coma. Deaths, though extremely rare, have been documented. Treatment for the bite might include the use of ice to slow the action of the toxin, excision of the wound, although that treatment has recently come into question, and treatment with antibiotics and other medications. An antivenin can be effective but is not often available.

Because many benign spider bite symptoms resemble the bite of the brown recluse, it is important, if possible, to save the captured or killed spider for identification. This helps ensure proper diagnosis and appropriate treatment.

## Scorpion

You've probably seen it in a movie: At a bar in Mexico, two macho types make a bet. The loser has to dance with a scorpion, and is dead in a few minutes. Although in real life the death would probably have taken several hours,

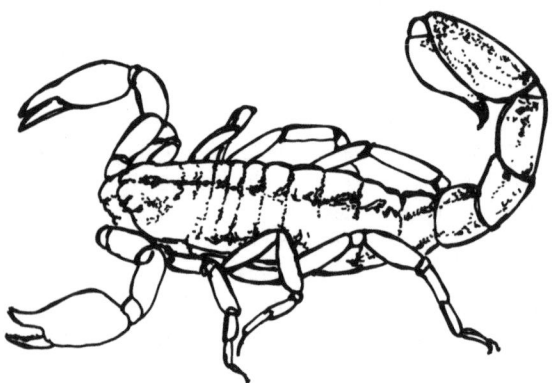

Scorpions can be identified by their distinctive shape.

the notion confirms personal observation: Scorpions look deadly. They are a ghoulish yellow, have pincers and stingers, and seem to move with the speed of a deadly bullet. Some are tiny, 2 centimeters, but they can be up to 10 centimeters, and they all seem to prefer to walk across the bedroom floor at night, as though they know people might be about with bare feet.

While it is prudent, at the least, to know about and understand scorpions where you live or travel, only one of our one hundred or so species has venom that puts us at true risk. *Centruroides exilicauda* (aka *C. sculpturatus*) is a resident of Arizona and New Mexico, and perhaps the California side of the Colorado River.[2] It is a small scorpion, about 2 centimeters long, is yellow to yellowish brown, and is commonly called the bark scorpion because it likes to hang out under tree bark. It can cause death, probably due to respiratory paralysis and other complications, usually within one and one-half to forty-two hours. Children are especially at risk.

*Black Widow Spiders, Brown Recluse Spiders, Bark Scorpions:\* Appropriate Immediate Response to Venomous Bites*

- If possible, capture or kill the spider or scorpion and put it in a container. Even if it appears to be dead, do not handle it with bare hands. Rather, scoop it up with a piece of paper. Take it with you when you go for treatment; identification can contribute to successful treatment.

- Seek immediate medical care even if the bite or sting does not feel severe. Quick medical attention, especially for bark scorpion bites, has reduced the death rate from such bites almost to zero, and has especially benefited children.

- If you cannot get to a medical facility quickly, call a poison control hot line. You can get this number locally by calling 911.

- Do not attempt home treatments other than staying calm and applying an ice pack to the wound (which slows absorption of venom).

- If the victim is a child, is elderly, or is in ill health, consider the bite an urgent medical emergency. Most deaths from bark scorpion bites occur in children.

\*Bites by other U.S. scorpions are not generally dangerous.

The sting of the bark scorpion is noticed immediately and can cause numbness or tingling at the site of the sting, with no swelling. Other symptoms to watch for, especially in children, are restlessness and jerky movement of the head, neck, and eyes. Symptoms in adults include increased heart and breathing rates, and breathing difficulties. The presence of any of these symptoms, or of failure to respond, especially in children, requires prompt action. A near-zero fatality rate for bark scorpion bites has been achieved only through prompt medical intervention.

First aid for a bark scorpion bite includes keeping the victim calm, "to minimize absorption of the venom," and applying a pressure dressing and cold pack to the sting. Treatment at the hospital might include the use of oxygen, breathing assistance, and pain relievers. Antivenins are available, but their usefulness as a routine response to a bite is debated. Antivenin should, however, "be given to all people who are unresponsive or have a severe reaction, particularly children."[3]

The sting of other U.S. scorpions is usually accompanied by pain, swelling, tenderness, and warmth at the site. (Note that bark scorpion bites do not usually swell, while other scorpion bites do.) These bites need not be treated as an emergency unless systemic symptoms are present. It is still a good idea, however, to call a poison control center to verify that symptoms experienced are benign. Some symptoms, such as muscle spasms, may occur and can benefit from medical treatment. Otherwise home treatment is acceptable and might include the use of ice packs, antihistamine and analgesic ointments, and bed rest.

### Avoiding Spider Bites and Scorpion Stings

- Learn to recognize scorpions and venomous spiders in areas where you live or visit. Also learn the symptoms of their bites and stings, so you know when to seek immediate medical help.
- In areas where scorpions or venomous spiders are common, do not go barefoot—especially at night when scorpions and black widow spiders are active.
- Shake out clothing and check shoes before putting them on.

- Keep your house clean of bugs that are prey to scorpions and spiders. This will discourage them from hunting in your house.
- Seal cracks and other openings that make it easy for scorpions and spiders to enter your home.
- Learn to recognize the web of the black widow spider: unlike most other spiders, the web has an erratic, untidy shape.

## Chigger Mite

The skin affliction called "chiggers" is caused by the larval stage of the chigger mite. The larvae are tiny (0.2 millimeters long) and may be red, orange, or yellow. In the U.S., it is commonly the larval stage of *Eutrombicula alfreddugesi* that connects with humans. The adults do not bite us. *E. alfreddugesi* does not transmit disease, and chiggers are not contagious.

Chigger mites are found in most of the United States. They prefer moist grassy, weedy, or wooded areas and attach themselves to hosts, including humans, who brush

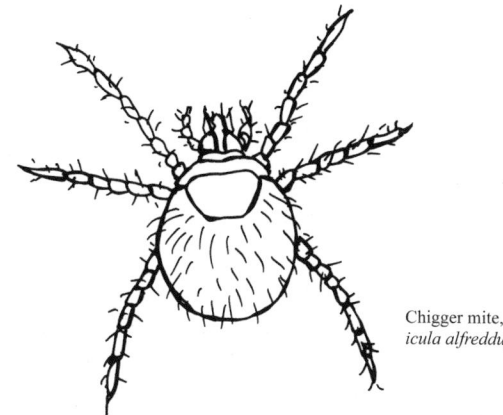

Chigger mite, *Entrombicula alfreddugesi,* larva.

by them. Once aboard, they search for areas where clothes fit tightly or the skin is tender, such as at the waistline or groin. Contrary to popular belief, they do not burrow into the skin. Rather, they insert their mouthparts into the skin and feed. They usually leave the host in a few days.

Unlike their relative the tick, chigger mites do not make a meal of the host's blood. Rather, the larvae inject saliva into the host, then ingest the resulting mixture of saliva and the host's cell tissue. Attached chiggers cause an intensely itchy rash.

Chigger infestations can be prevented or interrupted by bathing in hot soapy water, which should remove any chiggers. Treatment with antiseptic, anesthetic, anti-inflammatory, and analgesic ointments can relieve symptoms.

## Scabies Mite

*Sarcoptes scabiei*, the scabies mite, inhabits the globe worldwide. It is related to the mites that cause mange in animals. *S. scabiei* is very small (0.2 to 0.4 millimeters long), is host-specific, and relies on humans as hosts. It is contagious from person to person, and when it is not recognized and controlled immediately, it can spread through an entire household.

Signs of scabies infection may not appear until a month after infestation, when the human host becomes sensitized and develops an immune reaction. Symptoms include intense itching, and slightly raised wavy lines on the skin about 0.5-inch long, sometimes with a pimple at one end. The lines may be any place on the body, but areas with natural creases are favored. The lines are evidence of the burrows created by the female mites. Unlike chiggers, scabies do crawl into the skin, where they lay their eggs. The eggs hatch in a few days, emerge from the skin, and

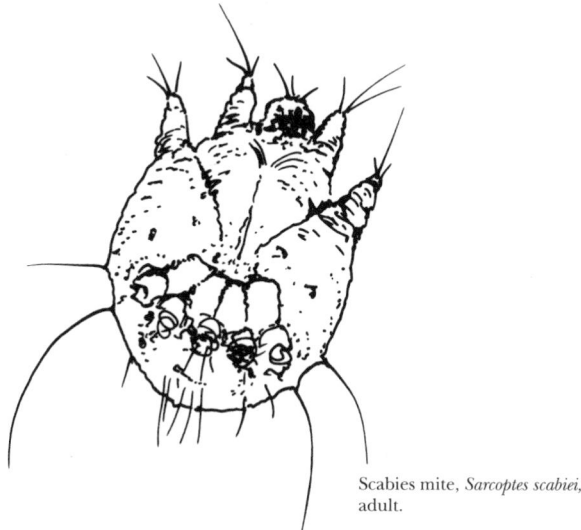

Scabies mite, *Sarcoptes scabiei*, adult.

molt through several stages into adults. The entire life cycle is carried out on human hosts and lasts only ten to seventeen days.

Although diagnosis based on symptoms—itching and burrows—is usually enough, it is a good idea to confirm the presence of scabies by inspecting scrapings from the burrows under a microscope. This rules out other dermatitis diagnoses. Treatment is with over-the-counter scabicide creams containing permethrin, lindane, or a similar ingredient. The cream is applied and left on the skin for fourteen to forty-eight hours (follow instructions in the packet). After that, a bath may be taken. Although itching may persist for another week, treatment is usually successful. After treatment, corticosteroid creams may be used to reduce itching.

Because the scabies mite cannot live off human hosts for more than a day or so, it is not necessary to treat clothing, bedding, or rooms with insecticides. After treatment of people, however, clothing and bedding should be washed and heat-dried.

# Notes

Please refer to Works Cited (page 89) for full citation and for complete article page numbers.

### *Introduction*

1. Fraser.

### *Chapter 1: The Lyme Disease Saga*

1. National Institutes of Health, "NIAID Research: Antibiotic Therapy."

2. Cook, p. 152.

3. Keirans, p. 310.

4. Anderson, p. 217.

5. Anderson, p. 220.

6. Rahn, p. 2.

7. Lewis, Barbara A., p. 229.

8. Steere, p. 231.

9. Steere, p. 226.

### *Chapter 2: Blacklegged Ticks*

1. "Tick-Transmitted Diseases in Humans," p. 1.

2. Keirans, p. 311.

3. Steere, p. 222.

4. Centers for Disease Control and Prevention, "Lyme Disease: Introduction."

5. Steere, pp. 222–223.

6. Steere, pp. 222–223.

7. Steere, pp. 222–223.

### *Chapter 3: Lyme Disease*

1. Barbour, p. 47.

2. Aly, p. 163.

3. Strobino, p. 711.

4. Silver; Strobino.

5. Silver, p. 96.

6. American College of Physicians Online, "Lyme Disease: A Patient's Guide [Treatment]."

7. Rahn, pp. 61–63.

8. Anderson, p. 217.

9. Rahn, pp. 36–37.

10. Berkow, p. 880.

11. Rahn, p. 38.

12. National Institutes of Health, "Symptoms of Lyme Disease."

13. Rahn, p. 39.

14. Rahn, pp. 41–42.

15. Rahn, p. 43; Steere, p. 226.

16. "Memory, Mood & Lyme Disease."

17. "How Lyme Disease Is Diagnosed."

18. Food and Drug Administration, "FDA Talk Paper"; Lewis, p. 2.

19. Cook, p. 155.

20. "Lyme Disease," www.cdc.gov.

21. Steere, p. 228.

22. Henderson, "Dot Blot Test Detects Infection in Vaccine."

23. Schuster.

24. Food and Drug Administration, "Lyme Disease: Difficult to Diagnose."

25. Rahn, p. 50.

26. Rahn, p. 50.

27. "FDA Approves First Lyme Disease Vaccine."

28. National Institutes of Health, "NIH Chronic Lyme Disease Treatment Study Protocol."

29. National Institutes of Health, "NIAID Research: Antiobiotic Therapy."

30. Sanders.

31. Cook, p. 159.

32. Mlot.

33. Pound.

34. Bonagura, pp. 306–307.

35. Rahn, p. 27.

### *Chapter 4: Preventing Lyme Disease*

1. Steere, p. 231.

2. "Buzz Off!"

3. National Institutes of Health, "NIAID Research: Vaccine Production."

4. Barbour, p. 66.

### *Chapter 5: Other U.S. Tick-Borne Diseases*

1. Rahn, p. 51.

2. Centers for Disease Control and Prevention, "Lyme Disease: Questions and Answers."

3. "Recommendations for the Use of Lyme Disease Vaccine," p. 2.

4. National Institutes of Health, "Fact Sheet, Tick-Borne Diseases: An Overview for Physicians."

5. Busvine, pp. 82–83.

6. National Institutes of Health, "Fact Sheet, Tick-Borne Diseases: An Overview for Physicians."

7. National Institutes of Health, "NIAID-Supported Researchers Isolate Bacterium That Causes Potentially Deadly Tick-Borne Disease."

8. Barbour, p. 48.

9. National Institutes of Health, "Fact Sheet, Tick-Borne Diseases: An Overview for Physicians."

### *Chapter 7: Lyme Disease in Pets and Other Animals*

1. Bonagura, p. 307.

2. Bonagura, pp. 303–307.

### *Chapter 8: The Cousins: Black Widow and Brown Recluse Spiders, Scorpions, Chiggers, and Scabies*

1. Goddard, p. 278.

2. Berkow, p. 1365.

3. Berkow, p. 1365.

# Works Cited or Consulted

Aly, Raza, M.P.H., Ph.D., and Howard I. Maiback, M.D. *Atlas of Infections of the Skin.* Philadelphia: Churchill Livingstone, 1999.

American College of Physicians Online, www.acponline.org.

———. "Initiative on Lyme Disease." May 21, 2000, www.acponline.org/lyme/index.html.

———. "Initiative on Lyme Disease: A Patient's Guide [Diagnosis]." May 21, 2000, www.acponline.org/lyme/patient/diagnosis.htm.

———. "Lyme Disease: A Patient's Guide [Treatment]." May 21, 2000, www.acponline.org/lyme/patient/treatment.htm

Anderson, John F., and Louis A. Magnarelli. "Lyme Disease: A Tick-Associated Disease Originally Described in Europe, but Named After a Town in Connecticut." *American Entomologist,* winter 1994: 217–227.

"Attention Lyme Disease Sufferers!" April 30, 2000, www.lymealliance.org/Law_Firm/law_firm.html.

Barbour, Alan G., M.D. *Lyme Disease: The Cause, the Cure, the Controversy.* Baltimore: The Johns Hopkins University Press, 1996.

Barthold, Stephen W. "Globalization of Lyme Borreliosis." *The Lancet,* Vol. 348, No. 9042, Dec. 14, 1996: 1603 (2).

Berkow, Robert, M.D., Mark H. Beers, M.D., and Andrew F. Fletcher, M.B., B.Chir., eds. *The Merck Manual of Medical Information.* Whitehouse Station, New Jersey: Merck Research Laboratories, 1997.

*Black's Veterinary Dictionary.* Lanham, Maryland: Barnes & Noble Books, 1992.

Bonagura, John, *Kirk's Current Veterinary Therapy XII Small Animal Practice*. Philadelphia: W. B. Saunders Company, 1995.

Busvine, James R. *Disease Transmission by Insects*. New York: Springer-Verlag, 1993.

"Buzz Off!" Consumer Reports Online, June 2000, www.consumerreports.org.

Cacy, Jim, and James W. Mold. "The Clinical Characteristics of Brown Recluse Spider Bites Treated by Family Physicians. An OKPRN Study." *Journal of Family Practice*, Vol. 48, No. 7, July 1999: 536.

Centers for Disease Control and Prevention (CDC), www.cdc.gov.

Cook, Allan R., ed. *Arthritis Sourcebook*. 1st ed. Detroit: Omnigraphics, Inc., 1999.

De Kruif, Paul. *Microbe Hunters*. New York: Harcourt, Brace and Company, 1926.

Edelman, Daniel C., and J. Stephen Dumler. "Evaluation of an Improved PCR Diagnostic Assay for Human Granulocytic Ehrlichiosis." *Molecular Diagnosis*, Vol. 1, No. 1, 1996: 41.

Falco, Richard C., Donna F. McKenna, Thomas J. Daniels, Robert B. Nadelman, John Nowakowski, Durland Fish, and Gary P. Wormser. "Temporal Relation Between *Ixodes Scapularis* Abundance and Risk for Lyme Disease Associated with Erythema Migrans." *American Journal of Epidemiology*, Vol. 149, No. 8, 1999: 771–776.

"FDA Approves First Lyme Disease Vaccine." *HHS News* (U.S. Department of Health and Human Services), Dec. 21, 1998: 98–139, www.fda.gov.

Food and Drug Administration (FDA). www.fda.gov.

————. "FDA Talk Paper." July 4, 2000.

————. "Lyme Disease: Difficult to Diagnose." Center for Devices and Radiological Health, May 21, 2000.

Fraser, Claire M., et al. "Genomic Sequence of a Lyme Disease Spirochaete, *Borrelia burgdorferi.*" *Nature,* Vol. 390, 1997: 580.

Gelber, R. H. "Transmission of *Borrelia Burgdorferi* in *Ixodes Dammini.*" *Journal of Infectious Diseases,* 156(1): 234–239.

Goddard, Jerome. *Physician's Guide to Arthropods of Medical Importance.* New York: CRC Press, 1996.

Hawkins, David R., M.D., Ph.D. *Goodbye, Scorpion; Farewell, Black Widow Spider.* Sedona, Arizona: Veritas, 1996.

Henderson, Charles W. "Data Show Lyme Disease Vaccine Is Well Tolerated in Children." *Vaccine Weekly,* Dec. 13, 1999.

————. "Dot Blot Test Detects Infection in Vaccine." *Vaccine Weekly,* Jan. 19, 2000, www.pals.msus.edu.

————. "Spirochetes Identified in Taiwan." *World Disease Weekly Plus,* Jan. 25, 1999.

"How Lyme Disease Is Diagnosed." May 21, 2000, www.nih.gov.

Keirans, James E., H. Joel Hutcheson, Lance A. Durden, and J. S. H. Klompen. "*Ixodes (Ixodes) Scapularis* (Acari: Ixodidae): Redescription of All Active Stages, Distribution, Hosts, Geographical Variation, and Medical and Veterinary Importance." *Journal of Medical Entomology,* Vol. 33, No. 3, May 1996: 297–318.

Lang, Denise, with Joseph Territo, M.D. *Coping with Lyme Disease: A Practical Guide to Dealing with Diagnosis and Treatment.* 2nd ed. New York: Henry Holt and Company, 1997.

Lewis, Barbara A. "Prehistoric Juvenile Rheumatoid Arthritis in a Precontact Louisiana Population Reconsidered." *American Journal of Physical Anthropology,* Vol. 106, No. 2, June 1998: 229–248.

Lewis, Carol. "New Vaccine Targets Lyme Disease, New Hope for Diminishing 'Great Masquerader.'" *FDA Consumer Magazine* Publication No. (FDA) 99–1304, May–June 1999, www.fda.gov.

"Lyme Disease." Minnesota Department of Health, brochure IC#141–0596, November 1995.

"Memory, Mood & Lyme Disease." *Pediatrics for Parents,* Vol. 18, No. 5, May 1999: 2.

*The Merck Veterinary Manual.* Rahway, New Jersey: Merck & Co., 1991.

Mlot, Christine. "Biological Control for Deer Ticks." *Science News,* Aug. 9, 1997, Vol. 152, No.6: 89(1).

National Institutes of Health, www.nih.gov.

Nocton, James J., M.D., and Allen C. Steere, M.D. "Lyme Disease." *Advances in Internal Medicine,* Vol. 40, 1995: 69–117.

Palmer, E. Lawrence. *Fieldbook of Natural History.* New York: McGraw Hill Book Company, 1949.

Pound, J. Mathews. "Collaring Deer Ticks to Reduce Lyme Disease." *Agricultural Research,* Vol. 48, No. 1, Jan. 23, 2000.

Rahn, Daniel W., and Janine Evans. *Lyme Disease.* Philadelphia: American College of Physicians, 1998.

"Recommendations for the Use of Lyme Disease Vaccine: Recommendation of the Advisory Committee." *Morbidity and Mortality Weekly Report,* Vol. 48, No. RR7, June 4, 1999.

Sanders, Kay D., and Patrick G. Guilfoile. "New Records of the Blacklegged Tick, *Ixodes scapularis* (Acari: Ixodidae) in Minnesota." *Journal of Vector Ecology* Vol. 25, No. 2, 2000: 155–157.

"Scabies." Department of Medical Entomology, University of Sydney, Australia, June 28, 2000.

Schuster, Steven E. "*Borrelia Burgdorferi*–Specific Immune Complexes in Acute Lyme Disease." *Journal of the American Medical Association (JAMA),* Nov. 24, 1999, Vol. 282, No. 20: 1942.

Scott Morey, Sharon. "ACIP Issues Recommendations for Lyme Disease Vaccine." *American Family Physician,* Vol. 60, No. 7, Nov. 1, 1999: 2171.

"Second Opinion." *Mayo Clinic Newsletter,* Vol. 17, No. 6, June 1999: 8.

Seinost, Gerald. "Infection with Multiple Strains of *Borrelia Burgdorferi Sensu Stricto* in Patients with Lyme Disease" (abstract). *Journal of the American Medical Association (JAMA),* Vol. 283, No. 8, Feb. 23, 2000: 985.

Silver, Helayne M., M.D. "Lyme Disease During Pregnancy." *Infections in Obstetrics,* Vol. 11, No. 1, March 1997: 93–97.

Sonenshine, Daniel E. *Biology of Ticks,* Vol. 1. New York: Oxford University Press, 1991.

Sparano, Vin. T. "Private Lessons: Step-by-Step Instructions for the Sportsman." *Outdoor Life,* Vol. 199, No. 1, Jan. 1997: 83.

Stack, Lawrence B., M.D. "Images in Clinical Medicine: *Latrodectus mactans.*" *New England Journal of Medicine,* Vol. 336, No. 23, June 5, 1997: 1649 (l).

Steere, Allen C. "Lyme Disease." *Emerging Infections: Biomedical Research Reports.* Richard M. Krause, ed. New York: Academic Press, 1998: 219–238.

Strobino, Barbara, Ph.D., Syed Abid, Ph.D., and Michael Gewitz, M.D. "Maternal Lyme Disease and Congenital Heart Disease: A Case-Control Study in an Endemic Area." *American Journal of Obstetrics and Gynecology,* Vol. 100, March 1999: 711–716.

"Ticks." Department of Medical Entomology, University of Sydney, Australia, June 26, 2000.

Wormser, Gary P., M.D. "Vaccination as a Modality to Prevent Lyme Disease: A Status Report." *New Vaccines and Vaccine Technology,* Vol. 13, No. 1, March 1999: 135–148.

# Recommended Reading

Barbour, Alan G., M.D. *Lyme Disease: The Cause, the Cure, the Controversy.* Baltimore: The Johns Hopkins University Press, 1996.

De Kruif, Paul. *Microbe Hunters.* New York: Harcourt, Brace and Company, 1926.

Hawkins, David R., M.D., Ph.D. *Goodbye, Scorpion; Farewell, Black Widow Spider.* Sedona, Arizona: Veritas, 1996.

Guilfoile, Patrick, Ph.D. *Ticks Off! Controlling Ticks That Transmit Lyme Disease on Your Property.* Bemidji, Minnesota: ForSte Press, 2004.

Lang, Denise, with Joseph Territo, M.D. *Coping with Lyme Disease: A Practical Guide to Dealing with Diagnosis and Treatment.* 2nd ed. New York: Henry Holt and Company, 1997.

Rahn, Daniel W., and Janine Evans. *Lyme Disease.* Philadelphia: American College of Physicians, 1998.

# Index

# About the Author

Susan Carol Hauser teaches in the English Department at Bemidji State University in northern Minnesota. She has been a commentator on National Public Radio.

## Books by Susan Carol Hauser
### Natural History
*Wild Rice Cooking: History, Natural History, Harvesting, and Lore, with Recipes*
*Sugaring: A Maple Syrup Memoir*
*A Field Guide to Poison Ivy, Poison Oak, and Poison Sumac: Prevention and Remedies*

### Nonfiction
*You Can Write a Memoir*
*Full Moon: Reflections on Turning Fifty*
*Girl to Woman: A Gathering of Images*
*Which Way to Look*
*Meant to Be Read Out Loud*
*What the Animals Know*

### Poetry
*Outside after Dark: New & Selected Poems*
*Redpoll on a Broken Branch*

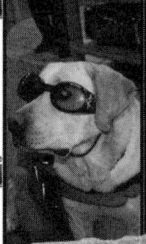